Better Homes and Gardens®
MAKE-AHEAD COOK BOOK

Above: Dazzle guests with tantalizing Rhubarb Cheesecake topped by a bright strawberry and rhubarb sauce. To complement the elegant dessert, add steaming cups of hot coffee.

On the cover: Creamy Ham Towers, Lime-Applesauce Mold, and Spiced Peaches are made ahead for a menu that is easy to serve, yet will win the approval of both family and guests.

BETTER HOMES AND GARDENS BOOKS

Editorial Director: Don Dooley
Managing Editor: Malcolm E. Robinson   Art Director: John Berg
Asst. Managing Editor: Lawrence D. Clayton   Asst. Art Director: Randall Yontz
Food Editor: Nancy Morton
Senior Food Editor: Joyce Trollope
Associate Editors: Rosemary C. Hutchinson, Sharyl Heiken
Assistant Editors: Sandra Mosley, Lorene Frohling,
Sandra Mapes, Elizabeth Strait, Catherine Penney, Elizabeth Walter
Designers: Julie Zesch, Harijs Priekulis, Faith Berven

CONTENTS

MAKE-AHEAD FAMILY MEALS

MAKE-AHEAD RECIPES

MAKE-AHEAD MEALS FOR ENTERTAINING

STORAGE TECHNIQUES

INDEX

Our seal assures you that every recipe in *Make-Ahead Cook Book* is endorsed by the Better Homes and Gardens Test Kitchen. Each recipe is tested for family appeal, practicality, and deliciousness.

THE ADVANTAGES OF MAKE-AHEAD COOKING

Do you come home from a busy day at the office or a club meeting to face a hungry family? Do the children need your attention just when it is time to start dinner? Or, would your husband like you to relax and talk with him before dinner, but you never have time? If so, you are among the many homemakers who are confronted with the problem of whether to have more time with their families or to serve delicious, home-cooked meals. There is a way to do both.

By reorganizing your meal preparation and doing most of the cooking ahead during less rushed hours, you can have more time for other activities. Not only will your family be getting attention when they need it, but they will have tasty meals, too. And you'll have time to enjoy both creative cookery and caring for the needs of your family.

Actually, the mechanics of make-ahead cooking are simple. Just shift meal preparation to a part of the day when you have more time, store the food, and then with a minimum of effort, complete the preparation for serving.

If you are a busy mother, maybe you have more time to cook while the children are napping or away at school. If you work outside the home or devote a lot of time to outside activities, you may prefer to prepare a few recipes ahead while cleaning up after a meal or to cook several dishes ahead on the weekends. And during warm weather, you may decide to prepare dinner during the morning.

Once the make-ahead preparation is done, you must store the food properly so your efforts won't be wasted. Refer to the last chapter in this book for complete details on refrigerating and freezing make-ahead dishes.

When serving time arrives, take out your make-ahead food and complete the last-minute steps. Add simple-to-prepare dishes to round out the menu, and call the family to the table. You'll be glad when everyone (including you) is relaxed and fresh to enjoy the meal, which is ready quickly, yet includes favorite, home-cooked dishes.

Planning the menu: As the name suggests, make-ahead menus must be planned in advance so the preparation can be done ahead. For family menus, select one or two make-ahead recipes and add simple dishes. For entertaining, choose a complete make-ahead menu so that most of the preparation is done in advance. To get you started, note the menus on the following pages for family meals and special occasions.

Organizing the preparation: Once you've decided on the menu, you will find it helpful to make a time schedule. For the more experienced homemakers, this may be only thinking through the schedule, but others will find it helpful to write down the steps, especially for parties and holidays.

By having such a plan, you can be confident that everything will be ready on time, and you will avoid anxiety that some important step will not be started on time or a dish will be forgotten. A written plan is also good if you must leave instructions for a child or your husband to begin the meal before you return home.

To aid you in organizing meal preparations, a time schedule is given with each menu in this book. These schedules—called Countdown from Kitchen to Table—include directions for the steps to be done in advance and a minute-by-minute schedule for the time just before serving the meal.

Using make-ahead recipes: The recipes in this book may be the beginning of your repertoire of make-ahead ideas. As you become oriented to making ahead, you may wish to add other recipes to those included here. Some of the family's favorite dishes or an interesting new recipe may be suitable to convert to make-ahead. To find out if the recipe is adaptable, check the storage charts in the last chapter to see if the food can be stored and for how long. Next, select a logical division in the preparation of the recipe between what can be done ahead and what should be left until serving time. The tip boxes at the end of each chapter in this book will offer helpful hints for making ahead, too.

COVER MENU

Creamy Ham Towers*
Spiced Peaches*
Lime-Applesauce Mold*
Quick Tortoni Cups*
Coffee   Milk
See index listing for page number.

COUNTDOWN FROM KITCHEN TO TABLE

Several days before the dinner, prepare Quick Tortoni Cups and freeze; prepare Spiced Peaches and refrigerate. Day before the dinner, prepare Lime-Applesauce Mold and Creamy Ham Towers; refrigerate.

Time before serving:

35 minutes	Bake patty shells.
15 minutes	Start coffee. Set table.
10 minutes	Heat main dish.
5 minutes	Pour beverage. Put food in serving dishes; set on table.

Serve dinner.

GUIDE TO RECIPE TIMINGS

The recipe timings given with each recipe in this book are defined as follows:

Minutes to Assemble—The approximate time needed to complete food preparation before final cooking or serving (does not include time spent in advance preparation).
Minutes Cooking Time—The approximate time needed for baking or heating food just before serving (does not include time spent in advance preparation). During this time, your attention is not usually required.
No Final Preparation—The food is completely prepared in advance; the only time required is that needed for serving the food.

make-ahead Family Meals

Giving the family a nutritious and tasty meal when time is short is difficult for most homemakers. Avoid this problem by following the directions for preparing meals ahead in these pages. Just use your spare time to make ahead, and store the foods in your refrigerator or freezer. Included in this section are ideas for breakfast, lunch, and dinner menus to make ahead, complete with a step-by-step plan for each menu to help you prepare the meal quickly.

Peppy Lasagna needs only to be baked and it's ready to serve. Meanwhile, reheat Freezer Garlic Bread and make a tossed salad.

MENUS TO START THE DAY

MENU

Chilled Fruit Compote
Bacon
Orange French Toast   Orange Syrup
or
Waffles   Orange Waffle Sauce
Milk   Coffee

COUNTDOWN
FROM KITCHEN TO TABLE

Prepare French toast *or* waffles; freeze. The day before serving, prepare Orange Syrup *or* waffle sauce and Chilled Fruit Compote; cover and refrigerate.

Time before serving:

15 minutes Bake Orange French Toast *or* Waffles. Start coffee.

10 minutes Fry bacon. Set table.

5 minutes Heat Orange Syrup *or* Orange Waffle Sauce. Pour beverages. Place foods in serving dishes and arrange on table.

Serve breakfast to family.

ORANGE SYRUP
5 minutes cooking time

1 cup light corn syrup
1 teaspoon grated orange peel
¼ cup orange juice

Advance preparation: Combine all ingredients; simmer 5 minutes. Cool. Store in covered container in refrigerator.
Before serving: Heat syrup. Serve over French toast or waffles. Makes 1¼ cups.

ORANGE FRENCH TOAST
5 minutes to assemble
10 minutes cooking time

2 eggs
1 cup orange juice
1 tablespoon sugar
¼ teaspoon salt
12 slices French bread
6 tablespoons butter or margarine

Advance preparation: Beat together eggs, orange juice, sugar, and salt. Dip bread into egg mixture, coating both sides. Place bread on baking sheets; freeze just till firm. Wrap and return to freezer.
Before serving: Place bread slices in well-buttered shallow baking pan. Melt butter; drizzle over bread. Bake at 500° for 5 minutes. Turn and bake till golden, about 5 minutes more. Makes 6 servings.

ORANGE WAFFLE SAUCE
5 minutes cooking time

2 oranges
Orange juice
½ cup sugar
2 tablespoons cornstarch
¼ teaspoon salt
1 cup water
2 tablespoons butter or margarine
1 teaspoon lemon juice

Advance preparation: Peel oranges over bowl. Section fruit and chop. Drain, reserving juice. To reserved juice, add additional orange juice to make ½ cup. In saucepan combine sugar, cornstarch, and salt. Add orange juice and water. Bring to boiling; reduce heat and simmer 3 minutes, stirring constantly. Blend in butter, lemon juice, and orange pieces. Cover; chill.
Before serving: Heat sauce; thin with additional orange juice, if desired.

WAFFLES
15 minutes cooking time

1¾ cups sifted all-purpose flour
3 teaspoons baking powder
½ teaspoon salt
2 beaten egg yolks
1¾ cups milk
½ cup salad oil
2 stiffly beaten egg whites

Advance preparation: Sift together flour, baking powder, and salt. Combine yolks, milk, and salad oil; stir into dry ingredients. Fold in beaten egg whites, leaving a few fluffs. Bake in preheated waffle baker; cool. Place waxed paper between waffles; wrap and freeze.
Before serving: Bake frozen waffles at 325° for 15 minutes or heat in toaster. Makes three 10-inch waffles.

CHILLED FRUIT COMPOTE
No final preparation

1 10-ounce package frozen raspberries, thawed
1 17-ounce can apricot halves
2 teaspoons cornstarch
Dash salt
1 17-ounce can purple plums

Advance preparation: Drain raspberries and apricot halves, reserving syrups. Combine raspberry and apricot syrups; add enough water to make 1½ cups liquid. In saucepan blend cornstarch and salt. Stir in syrup mixture. Cook and stir till thick and bubbly; cook and stir 3 minutes more. Drain plums. Add plums, raspberries, and apricots. Cover; chill thoroughly.
Before serving: Spoon fruit into serving dishes. Makes 6 to 8 servings.

Make use of leftover French bread by dipping slices in egg batter and freezing. When ready to serve, bake Orange French Toast and serve it topped with a pat of butter and Orange Syrup.

MENU

Apricot Drink
Canadian Bacon   Eggs in Tomato Shells
Apple-Nut Coffee Cake
Milk   Coffee

COUNTDOWN
FROM KITCHEN TO TABLE

Prepare coffee cake; freeze. Day before serving, complete advance preparation for Eggs in Tomato Shells and Apricot Drink.

Time before serving:

40 minutes Complete the preparation of Eggs in Tomato Sauce.

30 minutes Heat Apple-Nut Coffee Cake. Start coffee. Set table.

10 minutes Cook Canadian-style bacon.

5 minutes Pour beverages. Put food in dishes; set on table.

Serve brunch to the family.

EGGS IN TOMATO SHELLS
5 minutes to assemble
35 minutes cooking time

Advance preparation: Using 4 medium-ripe (but firm) tomatoes, cut thin slice from top of each tomato; scoop out pulp. Drain 10 minutes. Sprinkle tomatoes with salt, pepper, and ½ teaspoon dried basil leaves, crushed. Arrange in baking dish, cut side up. Cover and refrigerate.

Combine 1 ounce process Swiss cheese, shredded (¼ cup); ¼ cup fine dry bread crumbs; and 2 tablespoons butter or margarine, melted. Wrap and refrigerate.
Before serving: Break one egg into each tomato shell; sprinkle with salt. Bake at 350° till egg whites are set, about 35 minutes. Sprinkle crumb mixture over eggs. Bake till cheese melts. Makes 4 servings.

APPLE-NUT COFFEE CAKE
30 minutes cooking time

¼ **cup shortening**
½ **cup granulated sugar**
1 **egg**
½ **teaspoon vanilla**
1 **cup sifted all-purpose flour**
1 **teaspoon baking powder**
¼ **teaspoon baking soda**
⅛ **teaspoon salt**
½ **cup dairy sour cream**
¾ **cup finely chopped, peeled apple**
¼ **cup chopped nuts**
¼ **cup brown sugar**
½ **teaspoon ground cinnamon**
1 **tablespoon butter or margarine, melted**

Advance preparation: In mixing bowl cream shortening and granulated sugar together. Add egg and vanilla; beat well. Sift flour, baking powder, soda, and salt together; add to creamed mixture alternately with sour cream. Fold in apple. Spread batter in greased 8x8x2-inch baking pan. Combine nuts, brown sugar, cinnamon, and butter. Sprinkle over batter. Bake at 350° for 30 to 35 minutes. Cool 10 minutes; remove from pan. Cool thoroughly. Wrap coffee cake in foil and freeze.
Before serving: Heat frozen coffee cake in foil wrap at 350° till warm through, about 30 minutes. Open foil wrap during last 10 minutes of heating.

APRICOT DRINK
No final preparation

1 **12-ounce can apricot nectar**
1 **cup orange juice**
3 **tablespoons lime juice**
  Dash ground nutmeg (optional)

Advance preparation: Blend together apricot nectar, orange juice, and lime juice. Cover and chill thoroughly.
Before serving: Pour apricot mixture into small glasses; sprinkle with a dash of nutmeg, if desired. Makes 4 servings.

MENU

Stewed Apples
Cornmeal Scrapple   Poached Eggs
Orange-Cinnamon Rolls *or* Toast
Milk   Coffee

COUNTDOWN
FROM KITCHEN TO TABLE

Prepare rolls and freeze. Day before serving, prepare scrapple and Stewed Apples.

Time before serving:

20 minutes Cook Cornmeal Scrapple.

15 minutes Heat rolls. Make coffee. Set table.

10 minutes Poach eggs. Prepare toast.

5 minutes Pour beverages. Put food in serving dishes; set on table.

Serve breakfast to family.

CORNMEAL SCRAPPLE

5 minutes to assemble
20 minutes cooking time

  1 cup cornmeal
  1 cup milk
  1 teaspoon sugar
  1 teaspoon salt
  8 ounces bulk pork sausage, cooked
    All-purpose flour
  2 tablespoons butter or margarine

Advance preparation: Combine cornmeal, milk, sugar, and salt. Gradually stir into 2¾ cups boiling water; cook and stir till thick. Cook, covered, over *low* heat 10 to 15 minutes. Finely crumble sausage; add to cornmeal mixture. Pour into 7½x3¾x2¼-inch loaf pan. Cover; chill.
Before serving: Cut scrapple into ½-inch slices; dip in flour. Fry slowly in butter for 15 to 20 minutes. Makes 6 servings.

STEWED APPLES
No final preparation time

  1 8-ounce package dried apples
  2 cups water
  1 cup orange juice
  1 tablespoon lemon juice
  ½ cup maple-flavored syrup

Advance preparation: Rinse apples; put in 3-quart saucepan. Add water, orange juice, and lemon juice. Simmer, covered, 20 to 30 minutes. During last 5 minutes, add maple-flavored syrup. Cover and chill.
Before serving: Ladle stewed apples into small bowls. Makes 6 to 8 servings.

ORANGE-CINNAMON ROLLS

5 minutes to assemble
15 minutes cooking time

  1 13¾-ounce package hot roll mix
  ¼ cup butter or margarine, softened
  ½ cup granulated sugar
  1 tablespoon grated orange peel
  ½ teaspoon ground cinnamon
  ¼ teaspoon ground nutmeg
  1 cup sifted confectioners' sugar
  2 tablespoons orange juice

Advance preparation: Prepare roll mix according to package directions. After dough has risen once, punch down and knead 3 or 4 times on lightly floured surface. Roll dough to 24x18-inch rectangle. Spread softened butter over dough.
  Blend granulated sugar, orange peel, cinnamon, and nutmeg. Sprinkle over dough. Roll jelly-roll fashion, beginning with long side; seal edges. Cut into 1-inch slices; place, cut side down, on greased baking sheet. Cover; let rise till double, 30 to 40 minutes. Bake at 375° for 18 to 20 minutes. Cool on rack. Divide rolls into family-sized portions; wrap in foil. Freeze.
Before serving: Heat frozen rolls in foil wrap at 325° for 15 minutes. Meanwhile, combine confectioners' sugar and orange juice. Just before serving, drizzle over hot rolls. Makes 2 dozen rolls.

LUNCH MENUS

MENU

Tomato Refresher
Chicken Stack-Ups
Relish Tray
Pineapple Pie *or* Golden Sundaes
Milk   Coffee

COUNTDOWN
FROM KITCHEN TO TABLE

Prepare main dish and freeze. Day before serving, make Tomato Refresher and Pineapple Pie or Golden Sundaes; chill.

Time before serving:

40 minutes Bake Chicken Stack-Ups.

15 minutes Prepare relish tray. Start coffee. Set table.

10 minutes Complete preparation for Chicken Stack-Ups.

5 minutes Pour beverage. Put food in serving dishes; set on table.

Serve lunch to the family.

GOLDEN SUNDAES
5 minutes final preparation

Advance preparation: In saucepan combine ½ cup sugar, 2 tablespoons cornstarch, and ⅛ teaspoon ground cinnamon. Gradually blend in 2 cups apricot nectar; add 1 teaspoon grated orange peel. Cook and stir till thick and bubbly. Remove from heat. Stir in 4 or 5 fresh, medium apricots, cut in chunks (1 cup). Cover; chill thoroughly.
Before serving: Scoop vanilla ice cream into dessert dishes. Ladle chilled apricot sauce over top. Makes 8 servings.

TOMATO REFRESHER
No final preparation

  1 16-ounce can clam-tomato juice cocktail
  1 tablespoon lemon juice
  ½ teaspoon Worcestershire sauce
  ⅛ teaspoon celery salt

Advance preparation: Combine all ingredients; blend together thoroughly. Chill.
Before serving: Stir juice mixture; pour into chilled glasses. Makes 6 servings.

PINEAPPLE PIE
No final preparation

  1⅓ cups flaked coconut
  2 tablespoons butter or margarine, melted
  1 3¼-ounce package vanilla tapioca pudding mix
  1 3-ounce package lemon-flavored gelatin
  1¼ cups milk
  ½ of a 6-ounce can frozen unsweetened pineapple juice concentrate, thawed (⅓ cup)
  1 2- or 2⅛-ounce package dessert topping mix
  1 8¾-ounce can crushed pineapple, well drained

Advance preparation: Combine coconut and butter; press on bottom and sides of 9-inch pie plate. Bake at 325° till coconut is golden, about 15 minutes. Cool.
  In medium saucepan combine pudding mix and gelatin. Stir in milk. Cook and stir till mixture boils; remove from heat. Stir in concentrate; chill till partially set. Prepare dessert topping mix according to package directions. Fold into pudding mixture; add crushed pineapple. Pour into coconut shell; chill thoroughly.

CHICKEN STACK-UPS

10 minutes to assemble
40 minutes cooking time

1 2½-ounce package sour cream
　　sauce mix
1⅓ cups milk
1¼ cups finely chopped, cooked
　　chicken
2 tablespoons chopped green pepper
　　• • •
½ cup sifted all-purpose flour
½ teaspoon baking soda
1 slightly beaten egg
　　• • •
1 2¼-ounce package cheese sauce
　　mix
1 8-ounce can jellied cranberry
　　sauce, diced

Advance preparation: Prepare sour cream sauce mix according to package directions, using the 1⅓ cups milk. Combine ½ cup of the sour cream sauce, the chicken, and green pepper; set mixture aside.

Sift together flour and baking soda. Combine egg and remaining sour cream sauce. Stir flour mixture into egg mixture. Bake batter on hot griddle, using about 2 tablespoons mixture for each pancake. Place *half* of the pancakes in a 15½x10½x1-inch baking pan. Spread each with ¼ cup chicken mixture. Top with remaining pancakes. Cover tightly and freeze.

Before serving: Bake frozen stack-ups, covered, at 350° for 40 minutes. Prepare cheese sauce mix according to package directions. Spoon over pancakes. Top with diced cranberry sauce. Serves 6.

Chicken Stack-Ups is an easy dish to make using convenience products. Sour cream sauce mix flavors the chicken filling and pancakes, while cheese sauce mix completes the topping.

MENU

Toasted Cheese Sandwiches
Tomato-Lima Chowder
Chocolate Cups   *or*   Butterscotch Bars
Milk   Tea

COUNTDOWN
FROM KITCHEN TO TABLE

Prepare chowder and Chocolate Cups *or* Butterscotch Bars. Cover and freeze.

Time before serving:

30 minutes Begin heating Tomato-Lima Chowder.

15 minutes Prepare beverage. Set table.

10 minutes Prepare toasted cheese sandwiches.

5 minutes Pour beverage. Put food in serving dishes; set on table.

Serve lunch to the family.

BUTTERSCOTCH BARS
No final preparation

   1½ cups sifted all-purpose flour
   ¾ cup brown sugar
   6 tablespoons butter or margarine, softened
   1 6-ounce package butterscotch pieces (1 cup)
   ¼ cup light corn syrup
   1 cup coarsely chopped walnuts

Advance preparation: Combine flour, sugar, 4 *tablespoons* butter, and ¼ teaspoon salt. Press into 13x9x2-inch baking pan. Bake at 375° for 15 minutes. Combine butterscotch, syrup, remaining butter, 1 tablespoon water, and ½ teaspoon salt. Cook and stir over low heat till smooth. Add nuts; pour over first layer. Bake 8 minutes more. Cool; cut into bars. Wrap; freeze. Makes 48 bars.

TOMATO-LIMA CHOWDER
30 minutes cooking time

   2 chicken bouillon cubes
   1 16-ounce can tomatoes, cut up
   1 10-ounce package frozen lima beans
   1 10-ounce package frozen whole kernel corn
   ⅓ cup chopped onion
   2 tablespoons snipped parsley
   1 clove garlic, minced
          • • •
   1 cup milk
   ¼ cup all-purpose flour
   ½ teaspoon salt
   ⅛ teaspoon dried thyme leaves, crushed
   Dash ground nutmeg
   2 tablespoons butter or margarine

Advance preparation: Dissolve bouillon cubes in 1 cup hot water. Add tomatoes, beans, corn, onion, parsley, and garlic. Cover; bring to boiling. Simmer 20 minutes. In screw-top jar combine milk, flour, salt, thyme, nutmeg, and dash pepper. Cover; shake. Stir into vegetable mixture; bring to a boil. Cook and stir till thick and bubbly. Add butter; cool quickly. Freeze in three 1-pint freezer containers.

Before serving: Remove chowder from containers. Heat in saucepan till hot, about 30 minutes. Stir often. Makes 6 servings.

CHOCOLATE CUPS
No final preparation

   1 6¾-ounce package instant chocolate pudding mix
   2 tablespoons sugar
   1 tablespoon instant coffee powder
   ¼ cup chopped almonds, toasted

Advance preparation: Prepare pudding according to package directions, adding sugar and coffee powder to dry mix. Stir in chopped almonds. Spoon into 8 paper bake cups in muffin pans. Freeze. Remove frozen desserts from muffin pans; wrap and return to freezer. Makes 8 servings.

COUNTDOWN
FROM KITCHEN TO TABLE

Make Biscuits and freeze. The day before serving, prepare Turkey in Aspic; chill.

Time before serving:

25 minutes Bake Biscuits. Set table.

10 minutes Slice tomatoes. Prepare tea.

5 minutes Pour beverage. Put foods in serving dishes; set on table.

Serve lunch to family.

BISCUITS
25 minutes cooking time

2 cups sifted all-purpose flour
3 teaspoons baking powder
½ teaspoon salt

• • •

¼ cup shortening
¾ cup skim milk

Advance preparation: Sift dry ingredients into bowl. Cut in shortening till like coarse crumbs. Make a well in center; add milk. Stir quickly with fork just till dough follows fork around bowl. Turn onto floured surface. Knead gently 10 to 12 strokes. Roll dough ½ inch thick. Dip cutter in flour; cut straight down without twisting. Put biscuits on baking sheet; freeze just till firm. Wrap; freeze.
Before serving: Bake frozen biscuits on *ungreased* baking sheet at 425° for 20 to 25 minutes. Makes 16. (86 calories/biscuit.)

TURKEY IN ASPIC
5 minutes final preparation

Advance preparation: Trim 6 slices cooked turkey (¼ inch thick) to uniform shapes. Blend together one 2½-ounce can deviled ham, 1 tablespoon snipped parsley, 2 teaspoons finely chopped onion, and 1 teaspoon prepared horseradish. Spread meat slices with ham mixture. Slice 2 hard-cooked eggs; arrange 2 slices of egg atop each slice of turkey.

In saucepan soften 2 envelopes unflavored gelatin (2 tablespoons) in two 13¾-ounce cans chicken broth. Add ½ cup water, 2 slightly beaten egg whites, and 1 tablespoon lemon juice. Bring the mixture to boiling, stirring constantly. Remove from heat and strain through cheesecloth. Pour thin layer of aspic into 9x9x2-inch pan; chill till almost set. Arrange meat slices on aspic; carefully pour the remaining aspic over slices. Cover and chill till set.
Before serving: Trim aspic closely around each slice of meat. Arrange on lettuce. Makes 6 servings. (207 calories/serving.)

Low-calorie meals can be colorful and flavorful. For example, try Turkey in Aspic for a luncheon or light supper menu.

DINNER MENUS

COUNTDOWN
FROM KITCHEN TO TABLE

Prepare the meatballs; freeze them. The day before serving, prepare Fruited Nectar Salad, Dilled Cucumbers, and Creamy Bananas; cover and refrigerate.

Time before serving:

25 minutes Prepare Spicy Meatballs. Cook rice. Start coffee.

15 minutes Cook spinach. Set table.

5 minutes Pour beverages. Put food in serving dishes; set on table.

Serve dinner to the family.

DILLED CUCUMBERS
No final preparation

⅓ cup salad oil
3 tablespoons vinegar
½ teaspoon dried dillweed
½ teaspoon salt
¼ teaspoon sugar
⅛ teaspoon pepper

• • •

1 large cucumber, sliced thinly

Advance preparation: Blend together salad oil, vinegar, dillweed, salt, sugar, and pepper. Add cucumber. Chill thoroughly.

FRUITED NECTAR SALAD
No final preparation

1 12-ounce can apricot nectar
1 3-ounce package lemon-flavored gelatin
½ cup water
1 tablespoon lemon juice
1 11-ounce can mandarin orange sections, drained
½ cup halved, seedless grapes
¼ cup chopped, unpeeled apple
Mayonnaise or salad dressing

Advance preparation: Heat nectar to boiling. Add gelatin; stir till dissolved. Add water and lemon juice. Chill till partially set; fold in oranges, grapes, and apple. Pour into 4½-cup mold. Chill till firm.
Before serving: Unmold salad onto lettuce-lined plate, if desired. Serve with mayonnaise. Makes 4 to 6 servings.

CREAMY BANANAS
5 minutes final preparation

2 egg yolks
¼ cup sugar
1 teaspoon lemon juice
½ teaspoon vanilla
1 8-ounce package cream cheese, softened
3 tablespoons milk
3 bananas, sliced (about 3 cups)
½ of a 1-ounce square semisweet chocolate, grated

Advance preparation: Beat egg yolks, sugar, lemon juice, and vanilla till thick and lemon colored. Gradually beat in cream cheese till smooth and fluffy. Beat in milk. Chill mixture thoroughly.
Before serving: Spoon cream cheese mixture over sliced bananas; sprinkle with grated chocolate. Makes 6 servings.

SPICY MEATBALLS
10 minutes to assemble
15 minutes cooking time

    1 beaten egg
    1 6-ounce can evaporated milk
1½ cups soft bread crumbs
        (about 2 slices)
    ¼ cup chopped onion
    1 teaspoon salt
    ⅛ teaspoon ground nutmeg
        Dash pepper
1½ pounds ground beef
               • • •
    2 10¾-ounce cans beef gravy
    ¼ cup brown sugar
    2 tablespoons wine vinegar
    1 teaspoon ground ginger
    3 cups hot cooked rice

Advance preparation: Thoroughly combine beaten egg, evaporated milk, soft bread crumbs, chopped onion, salt, nutmeg, and pepper. Add ground meat; mix well. Shape the meat mixture into 30 balls (the mixture will be soft). Place meatballs in a 15½x 10½x2¼-inch baking pan. Bake at 375° till brown, 25 to 30 minutes.

Drain meatballs. Arrange meatballs on baking sheet and freeze just till firm. Wrap in foil or clear plastic bag; return meatballs to the freezer.

Before serving: In large skillet combine beef gravy, brown sugar, wine vinegar, and ginger. Bring mixture to boiling; add frozen meatballs. Cover and cook over low heat till heated through, about 15 minutes. Serve meatballs and gravy over hot cooked rice. Makes 6 servings.

Treat the family to a medley of fruit flavors with Fruited Nectar Salad. Apricot nectar, grapes, apples, and mandarin oranges blend together for a delicious, refreshing salad.

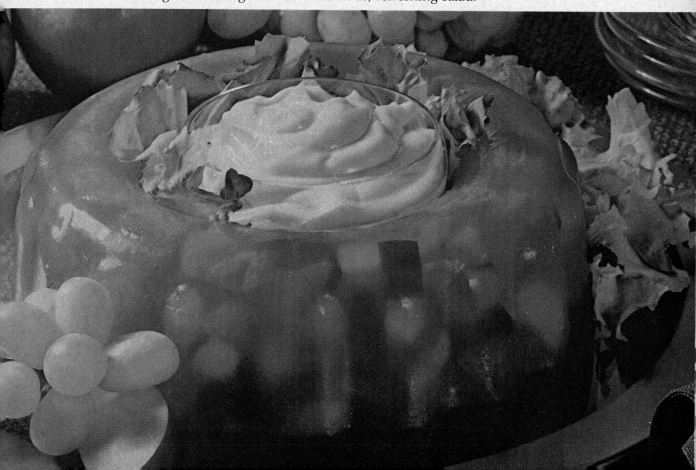

COUNTDOWN
FROM KITCHEN TO TABLE

Prepare Chicken and Rice Dish, Frozen Pineapple Salad, and Marble Squares; freeze. Day before serving, prepare Broccoli Bake and Fudge Sauce; cover; chill.

Time before serving:

1¾ hours   Bake main dish; thaw cake.

35 minutes Cook vegetable. Set table.

10 minutes Prepare salad and beverage.

5 minutes   Pour beverage. Put food in serving dishes; set on table.

Serve dinner to the family.

FROZEN PINEAPPLE SALAD
10 minutes final preparation

   1 3-ounce package cream cheese,
      softened
   1 8-ounce carton pineapple-flavored
      yogurt
   ¼ cup sugar
   1 8¾-ounce can crushed pineapple,
      drained
      Lettuce leaves
      Chopped nuts

Advance preparation: Blend together the cream cheese, yogurt, and sugar. Stir in pineapple. Spoon into 6 paper bake cups in muffin pan. Cover and freeze.
Before serving: Remove paper cups from salads. Arrange on lettuce leaves and top with chopped nuts, if desired. Let stand 10 minutes before serving. Serves 6.

CHICKEN AND RICE DISH
1¾ hours cooking time

   1 cup uncooked long-grain rice
   1 13¾-ounce can chicken broth
   1 10½-ounce can condensed cream
      of mushroom soup
   2 tablespoons chopped canned
      pimiento
   2 tablespoons sliced green onion
   1 2- to 3-pound ready-to-cook
      broiler-fryer chicken, cut up
      Paprika

Advance Preparation: Combine rice, broth, soup, ¼ cup water, pimiento, and onion. Turn into 13½x8¾x1¾-inch baking dish. Place chicken atop; season with salt and pepper. Cover; chill.
Before serving: Bake casserole, covered, at 350° for 1 hour. Stir rice; sprinkle chicken with paprika. Bake, uncovered, till tender, about 45 minutes more. Stir rice again before serving. Serves 4.

BROCCOLI BAKE
35 minutes cooking time

   1 10-ounce package frozen cut
      broccoli
   1 10½-ounce can condensed cream
      of mushroom soup
   2 ounces sharp process American
      cheese, shredded (½ cup)
   1 beaten egg
   ¼ cup mayonnaise or salad dressing
   ¼ cup milk
   1 tablespoon butter or margarine
   ¼ cup fine dry bread crumbs

Advance preparation: Cook broccoli according to package directions, *omitting salt*; drain thoroughly. Blend soup, cheese, and egg. Add mayonnaise and milk; stir in broccoli. Turn into 10x6x1¾-inch baking dish. Cover; chill. Melt butter; toss with crumbs. Wrap; chill.
Before serving: Top broccoli with crumbs. Bake, uncovered, at 375° till crumbs are browned, 30 to 35 minutes. Serves 4 to 6.

MARBLE SQUARES
5 minutes final preparation

   ¾ cup sugar
   ½ cup butter or margarine
   1½ teaspoons vanilla
   2 eggs
   ⅔ cup sifted all-purpose flour
   ½ teaspoon baking powder
   ¼ teaspoon salt
   1 1-ounce square unsweetened
      chocolate, melted
   Vanilla ice cream
   Fudge Sauce

Advance preparation: Cream sugar with butter; add vanilla. Add eggs, beating just till blended. Sift together flour, baking powder, and salt. Stir into creamed mixture. Spoon *half* of the batter into another bowl; stir chocolate into remaining batter.
   Drop chocolate batter, checkerboard-fashion, from tablespoon in greased 8x8x2-inch baking pan. Fill in spaces with light mixture. Zigzag batter with spatula to marble. *Do not overmix.* Bake at 350° till done, 25 to 30 minutes; cool. Wrap; freeze.
Before serving: Thaw cake; cut into squares. Top each square with a scoop of vanilla ice cream; drizzle with Fudge Sauce.

FUDGE SAUCE
No final preparation

   ¾ cup sugar
   3 tablespoons unsweetened cocoa
      powder
   Dash salt
   2 tablespoons water
   1 6-ounce can evaporated milk
   2 tablespoons butter or margarine
   1 teaspoon vanilla

Advance preparation: In saucepan combine sugar, cocoa, and salt. Blend in water; stir to dissolve cocoa. Add milk; bring to boiling. Boil gently till thick, 3 to 4 minutes; stir often. Remove from heat; add butter and vanilla. Cover and chill. If desired, serve warm. Makes 1 cup.

Ladle Fudge Sauce over scoops of vanilla ice cream and marbled cake for a dessert that will please both family and guests. For an extra touch, heat the Fudge Sauce to convert Marble Squares into a deluxe version of the popular hot fudge sundae.

MENU

Peppy Lasagna
Tossed Salad   Freezer Garlic Bread
Mock Tortoni
Coffee   Milk

COUNTDOWN FROM KITCHEN TO TABLE

Prepare Freezer Garlic Bread and Mock Tortoni; freeze. The day before serving dinner, prepare Peppy Lasagna; cover and refrigerate.

Time before serving:

65 minutes Bake Peppy Lasagna.

30 minutes Heat garlic bread.

15 minutes Start coffee. Set table.

10 minutes Remove lasagna from oven. Prepare tossed salad.

5 minutes Pour beverage. Put food in serving dishes; set on table.

Serve dinner to the family.

MOCK TORTONI
No final preparation

1 tablespoon butter or margarine
⅓ cup fine vanilla wafer crumbs
2 tablespoons flaked coconut, toasted
¼ teaspoon almond extract

• • •

1 pint vanilla ice cream, softened
¼ cup apricot preserves
1 tablespoon chopped almonds, toasted

Advance preparation: Melt butter; add crumbs, coconut, and almond extract. Put in 6 paper bake cups in muffin pan; top with ice cream and preserves. Garnish with almonds. Cover; freeze. Makes 6 servings.

PEPPY LASAGNA
55 minutes cooking time

¾ pound Italian sausage
¼ cup finely chopped onion
¼ cup finely chopped celery
¼ cup finely chopped carrot
1 7½-ounce can tomatoes, cut up
1 6-ounce can tomato paste
¾ cup water
½ teaspoon salt
1 teaspoon dried oregano leaves, crushed
12 ounces fresh ricotta or cream-style cottage cheese (1½ cups)
¼ cup grated Parmesan cheese
2 beaten eggs
2 tablespoons snipped parsley
6 ounces lasagna noodles, cooked and drained
6 ounces mozzarella cheese, thinly sliced

Advance preparation: Cook sausage, onion, celery, and carrot till meat is lightly browned. Drain off fat. Stir in tomatoes, tomato paste, water, salt, oregano, and ⅛ teaspoon pepper. Simmer, covered, 15 minutes, stirring occasionally.

Combine ricotta, Parmesan, eggs, parsley, and ⅛ teaspoon pepper. Place *half* the noodles in 11¾x7½x1¾-inch baking dish. Spread with *half* the cheese mixture; top with *half* the mozzarella, then *half* of the meat sauce. Repeat layers. Cover; chill.
Before serving: Bake, covered, at 375° for 30 minutes. Uncover; bake 25 minutes more. Let stand 10 minutes. Serves 6.

FREEZER GARLIC BREAD
30 minutes cooking time

Advance preparation: Cut 1 long loaf French bread in 1-inch slices, *cutting to, but not through* bottom. Blend ½ cup softened butter or margarine and ¼ teaspoon garlic powder. Spread between slices. Wrap the garlic bread in foil; freeze.
Before serving: Heat frozen bread at 375° for 30 minutes. Makes 6 servings.

LOW-CALORIE MENU

Barbecue Meat Loaves
Broccoli   Coleslaw
Frosty Compote
Skim Milk   Coffee

COUNTDOWN
FROM KITCHEN TO TABLE

Prepare Barbecue Meat Loaves and Frosty Compote; freeze. The day before serving, prepare Coleslaw; cover and chill. Thaw dessert 3 hours before dinner.

Time before serving:

45 minutes Bake Barbecued Meat Loaves.

30 minutes Set table.

15 minutes Prepare barbecue sauce.

10 minutes Cook broccoli. Start coffee.

5 minutes Pour beverages. Put food in serving dishes; set on table.

Serve dinner to the family.

FROSTY COMPOTE
No final preparation

3 medium peaches, peeled and
   sliced (2 cups)
1 cup strawberries, halved
1 cup low-calorie lemon-lime
   carbonated beverage
2 tablespoons sugar
1 teaspoon lemon juice
• • •
2 tablespoons flaked coconut

Advance preparation: Place peaches and strawberries in 1-quart freezer container. Blend carbonated beverage, sugar, and lemon juice; pour over fruit. Seal; freeze.
Before serving: Thaw 3 hours. Top with coconut. Serves 6. (50 calories/serving.)

BARBECUE MEAT LOAVES
5 minutes to assemble
45 minutes cooking time

1 beaten egg
½ cup skim milk
1 cup soft bread crumbs
   (about 1½ slices)
¼ cup chopped onion
1 teaspoon salt
½ teaspoon dried oregano leaves,
   crushed
1½ pounds ground beef
• • •
⅔ cup catsup
1 tablespoon brown sugar
1 tablespoon prepared mustard
1 tablespoon lemon juice
1 tablespoon Worcestershire sauce

Advance preparation: In mixing bowl combine egg, milk, bread crumbs, onion, salt, and oregano. Add ground beef and mix well. Divide mixture into 6 portions; shape into small loaves or pat into six 4½x2¾x2¼-inch loaf pans. Wrap and freeze.
Before serving: Bake meat loaves, uncovered, at 375° till done, 40 to 45 minutes. Combine catsup, brown sugar, mustard, lemon juice, and Worcestershire sauce. Bring to boiling. Spoon sauce over meat loaves during last 10 minutes of baking. Makes 6 servings. (255 calories/serving.)

COLESLAW
No final preparation

3 cups shredded cabbage
⅓ cup chopped green pepper
⅓ cup mayonnaise-type salad
   dressing
1 tablespoon vinegar
1 teaspoon sugar
½ teaspoon caraway seed
¼ teaspoon salt

Advance preparation: Combine cabbage and green pepper. Blend remaining ingredients together. Toss with vegetables. Cover; chill. Serves 6. (73 calories/serving.)

make-ahead Recipes

If you're looking for new recipes to tempt the family's appetite, and you want to be creative at the same time, sample the recipes included in this section. Select a make-ahead recipe for a main dish, salad, vegetable, relish, bread, or dessert to highlight the meal. Or put several recipes together for a complete make-ahead meal. You'll discover you have time to enjoy preparing food because the time-consuming steps are done long before the rush of getting the meal ready to serve.

Ham-Vegetable Strata combines ham, peas, bread, sauce, and cheese into one dish so the meal is prepared, baked, and served together.

MAIN DISHES MADE EASY

OVEN-BARBECUED RIBS
45 minutes cooking time

4 pounds pork spareribs
1 cup catsup
⅓ cup vinegar
⅓ cup brown sugar
3 tablespoons Worcestershire sauce
1 teaspoon dry mustard
1 teaspoon paprika
½ teaspoon chili powder
1 medium onion, thinly sliced
½ lemon, thinly sliced

Advance preparation: In Dutch oven add salted water to ribs to cover. Cover pan; simmer till almost tender, about 1 hour. Drain ribs; place in shallow baking pan.

In saucepan combine 1 cup water, ½ teaspoon salt, catsup, and next 6 ingredients. Bring to boiling. Cook and stir 5 minutes. Add onion and lemon. Cool. Spoon over ribs. Cover; chill up to 24 hours.
Before serving: Bake ribs, uncovered, at 350° for 45 minutes; baste often. Serves 4.

COLD BEEF PLATTER
5 minutes final preparation

Advance preparation: Roast one 2½- to 3-pound rolled beef rump roast on rack in shallow roasting pan at 325° till meat thermometer registers 140° (rare), 1½ to 2 hours. Cool. Cut into ¼-inch slices. Place in shallow dish. Drain one 14½-ounce can asparagus spears and one 3-ounce can sliced mushrooms; arrange over roast.

Blend 1⅓ cups salad oil; ½ cup vinegar; 2 cloves garlic, minced; 2 teaspoons sugar; 1½ teaspoons salt; 1½ teaspoons dry mustard; and dash pepper. Pour over meat. Cover; chill 2 to 24 hours.
Before serving: Drain marinade; arrange meat, asparagus, and mushrooms on platter. Garnish with cherry tomatoes. Serves 6.

SAUERBRATEN
20 minutes to assemble
1½ hours cooking time

2 cups water
½ cup dry red wine
½ cup red wine vinegar
1 onion, thinly sliced
4 whole cloves
4 whole peppercorns
2 bay leaves
1 2½-pound beef rump roast
• • •
2 tablespoons shortening
⅓ cup gingersnap crumbs (5 cookies)

Advance preparation: Combine water, wine, vinegar, onion, cloves, peppercorns, and bay leaves. Bring to boiling; simmer 5 minutes. Cool. Place roast in large bowl; pour wine mixture over roast. Turn roast to coat all sides; cover bowl tightly and place in refrigerator. Marinate 2 to 3 days, turning at least twice each day.
Before serving: Remove roast from marinade and pat dry with paper toweling. Strain marinade. In Dutch oven, brown the roast in hot shortening. Add the marinade and simmer, covered, till meat is tender, 1¼ to 1½ hours. Add more water, if needed.

Remove roast to platter. Pour remaining marinade into large measuring cup; skim off fat. Add enough water to measure 2 cups. Return marinade to Dutch oven; stir in gingersnap crumbs. Cook and stir till crumbs are dissolved and gravy thickens, about 5 to 10 minutes. Slice roast thin; serve with gravy. Makes 6 servings.

All-time favorites

For a delicious dinner menu, combine the →
spicy flavor of Oven-Barbecued Ribs with Cheesy Potato Salad (see *Salads* for recipe).

Spoon wine sauce over slices of Teriyaki Tenderloin, and add a special touch with a garnish of watercress and kumquats.

TERIYAKI TENDERLOIN
5 minutes to assemble
50 minutes cooking time

    ½ cup dry sherry
    ¼ cup soy sauce
    2 tablespoons dry onion soup mix
    2 tablespoons brown sugar
    1 2-pound beef tenderloin

Advance preparation: Combine first 4 ingredients. Place beef in plastic bag; set in deep bowl. Add marinade and close bag. Chill 8 to 24 hours. Occasionally, press bag against meat to distribute marinade.
Before serving: Remove meat from marinade; place on rack in roasting pan. Bake at 425° for 50 minutes; baste occasionally with *half* of the marinade. Bring rest of marinade and 2 tablespoons water to boiling; Slice meat; spoon sauce over. Serves 6 to 8.

HERBED ROUND STEAK
1 hour cooking time

    1 2-pound beef round steak, cut
        ¾ inch thick
    2 tablespoons salad oil
    1 medium onion, sliced
    1 10½-ounce can condensed cream
        of celery soup
    ¾ cup milk
    ¼ teaspoon dried thyme leaves,
        crushed
    ½ teaspoon dried oregano leaves,
        crushed

Advance preparation: Cut steak into 6 portions; trim fat. Season with ½ teaspoon salt and ⅛ teaspoon pepper. In skillet brown the steaks in hot oil; remove steaks. In same skillet brown onion. Return steaks to skillet; add ½ cup water. Simmer, covered, 1 hour. Remove steaks to 11¾x7½x1¾-inch baking dish; reserve drippings.
 Blend soup and milk; stir into reserved drippings. Add thyme and oregano. Pour over steaks. Cover; chill up to 24 hours.
Before serving: Bake, covered, at 350° till hot through, about 60 minutes. Serves 6.

ORANGE PORK CHOPS
45 minutes cooking time

Advance preparation: Trim fat from 6 pork chops, ¾ inch thick. Heat trimmings till 1 tablespoon fat accumulates; discard trimmings. Brown the chops in hot fat. Remove chops; season with 1 teaspoon salt and ⅛ teaspoon pepper. Drain skillet. In same skillet melt 3 tablespoons butter; blend in 3 tablespoons all-purpose flour. Add 1½ cups orange juice and ¼ cup water. Cook and stir till thick and bubbly. Add ¼ cup brown sugar and 1 tablespoon lemon juice. Return chops to skillet. Simmer, covered, 20 minutes. Put in 11¾x7½x1¾-inch baking dish. Place 1 thin onion slice and 1 orange slice on each chop. Cover; chill.
Before serving: Bake, covered, at 350° for 20 minutes. Uncover; bake 25 minutes longer, basting occasionally. Serves 6.

CHICKEN SUPREME
1 hour cooking time

¼ cup all-purpose flour
1 teaspoon paprika
3 large chicken breasts, skinned
¼ cup butter or margarine
2 tablespoons all-purpose flour
1¼ cups light cream
1 3-ounce can sliced mushrooms
1 tablespoon lemon juice
2 ounces process Swiss cheese, shredded (½ cup)

Advance preparation: Combine ¼ cup flour, paprika, 1 teaspoon salt, and dash pepper. Halve chicken breasts; coat with flour mixture. Brown in butter. Add 2 tablespoons water. Simmer, covered, 25 to 30 minutes. Remove chicken to an 11¾x7½x 1¾-inch baking dish; reserve drippings.
Combine 2 tablespoons flour, ½ teaspoon salt, and cream. Stir into reserved drippings in skillet. Cook and stir till thick and bubbly. Drain mushrooms; add mushrooms and lemon juice to sauce. Pour over chicken. Cover; chill up to 24 hours.
Before serving: Bake, covered, at 350° till hot through, 50 to 60 minutes. Sprinkle with cheese. Bake, uncovered, till cheese melts, 1 to 2 minutes. Makes 6 servings.

LIME CHICKEN
No final preparation

Advance preparation: Combine ½ cup salad oil, ½ teaspoon grated lime peel, ½ cup lime juice, 2 tablespoons snipped chives, ½ teaspoon salt, and 2 drops bottled hot pepper sauce. Place two 2- to 2½-pound ready-to-cook broiler-fryer chickens, cut up, in shallow pan. Pour marinade over chicken. Cover; chill 8 hours. Remove chicken; place, skin side down, in broiler pan. Broil 5 to 7 inches from heat till lightly browned, about 25 minutes. Brush chicken occasionally with marinade.
Turn and broil till done, 25 minutes more. Baste occasionally with marinade. Cover; chill up to 24 hours. Serves 6 to 8.

VEAL ITALIANO
30 minutes cooking time

1 tablespoon all-purpose flour
½ teaspoon salt
4 veal cutlets (1 pound)
2 tablespoons salad oil
1 8-ounce can tomatoes
1 6-ounce can tomato paste
½ cup water
1 3-ounce can sliced mushrooms, drained
½ cup red wine
⅓ cup sliced green onion
¼ cup sliced pitted ripe olives
¼ teaspoon garlic salt
¼ teaspoon dried basil leaves, crushed
Hot cooked noodles

Advance preparation: Combine flour, salt, and dash pepper; coat the veal with flour mixture. In skillet brown the veal slowly in hot oil. Drain off excess fat. Combine tomatoes and next 8 ingredients. Add to skillet. Cover; refrigerate up to 24 hours.
Before serving: Bring veal mixture to boiling; reduce heat and simmer, covered, till meat is tender, 25 to 30 minutes. Serve over hot noodles. Makes 4 servings.

SHISH KABOBS
25 minutes cooking time

½ cup Italian salad dressing
¼ cup lemon juice
1 teaspoon dried oregano leaves, crushed
¼ teaspoon salt
⅛ teaspoon pepper
2 pounds boneless lamb, cut in 2-inch cubes

Advance preparation: Blend dressing, lemon juice, oregano, salt, and pepper. Pour over lamb in shallow dish. Cover; chill 8 to 24 hours. Turn meat occasionally.
Before serving: Put meat on skewers; grill over *medium* coals 20 to 25 minutes. Turn occasionally; brush with marinade. Serves 5.

CHICKEN-ASPARAGUS BAKE
45 minutes cooking time

Excellent for company luncheon or dinner

>   2 large chicken breasts, cooked
>   (about 1 pound)
>   1 10-ounce package frozen asparagus
>   spears
>   • • •
>   ¼ cup butter or margarine
>   5 tablespoons all-purpose flour
>   1 cup milk
>   1 cup chicken broth
>   1 6-ounce can sliced mushrooms,
>   drained
>   ¼ teaspoon salt
>   ⅛ teaspoon ground nutmeg
>   Dash pepper
>   • • •
>   ¼ cup fine dry bread crumbs
>   2 tablespoons snipped parsley
>   2 tablespoons slivered almonds,
>   toasted
>   2 tablespoons butter or margarine,
>   melted

Advance preparation: Slice chicken breasts; set aside. Cook asparagus spears according to package directions; drain.

Melt the ¼ cup butter or margarine; blend in flour. Add milk and chicken broth all at once. Cook, stirring constantly, till the mixture is thickened and bubbly. Stir in sliced mushrooms, salt, ground nutmeg, and pepper. Arrange the chicken slices in the bottom of a 10x6x1¾-inch baking dish. Spoon *half* of the mushroom sauce over the chicken slices; arrange asparagus spears over sauce. Pour the remaining mushroom sauce over asparagus spears. Cover and refrigerate up to 24 hours.

Toss together dry bread crumbs, parsley, almonds, and 2 tablespoons melted butter or margarine. Place in covered container and refrigerate up to 24 hours.

Before serving: Bake chicken casserole, covered, at 375° for 30 minutes. Sprinkle crumb mixture atop casserole. Bake, uncovered, till heated through, about 15 minutes longer. Makes 4 servings.

HAM NEWBURG
20 minutes to assemble
15 minutes cooking time

>   1 cup all-purpose flour
>   ¼ teaspoon salt
>   ⅓ cup shortening
>   2 ounces process Swiss cheese,
>   shredded (½ cup)
>   Cold water
>   2 tablespoons chopped green pepper
>   6 tablespoons butter or margarine
>   3 tablespoons all-purpose flour
>   1½ cups light cream
>   • • •
>   3 tablespoons dry white wine
>   3 beaten egg yolks
>   2 cups cubed fully cooked ham
>   1 3-ounce can sliced mushrooms,
>   drained

Advance preparation: Sift together 1 cup flour and salt; cut in shortening till pieces are the size of small peas. Stir in cheese. Sprinkle cold water, 1 tablespoon at a time, over mixture, tossing gently with a fork. Repeat till all is moistened (using about 4 tablespoons water). Form into ball. Roll to ⅛-inch thickness; cut into four 6-inch circles. Fit into four 4½-inch tart pans, crimping edges high. Prick bottom and sides. Bake at 450° till golden, 12 to 14 minutes. Cool; remove pastry shells from pans. Cover loosely and store in refrigerator up to 24 hours.

In medium saucepan cook green pepper in butter or margarine till tender. Blend in 3 tablespoons flour. Add cream all at once. Cook and stir till thickened and bubbly. Remove from heat. Cover and store in refrigerator up to 24 hours.

Before serving: Warm pastry shells at 300°, uncovered, till hot, about 15 minutes.

Blend wine into creamed mixture. Cook and stir over medium heat till bubbly. Stir a moderate amount of hot mixture into egg yolks; return to mixture in saucepan. Stir in ham and mushrooms. Cook and stir over low heat just till mixture begins to bubble. Spoon newburg mixture into warm tart shells. Makes 4 servings.

CREAMY HAM TOWERS

10 minutes cooking time

As pictured on the front cover—

¼ cup butter or margarine
¼ cup all-purpose flour
1½ cups milk
1 chicken bouillon cube
2 ounces process American cheese, shredded (½ cup)
1 teaspoon prepared mustard
1 teaspoon Worcestershire sauce
2 cups cubed fully cooked ham
⅓ cup sliced, pitted ripe olives
2 tablespoons chopped canned pimiento
2 tablespoons snipped parsley
6 frozen patty shells, baked

Advance preparation: Melt butter; blend in flour. Add milk, ½ cup water, and bouillon cube. Cook and stir till thick and bubbly. Add cheese, mustard, and Worcestershire; stir till cheese melts. Add ham and next 3 ingredients. Cover; chill up to 24 hours.
Before serving: Heat ham mixture over low heat till hot through, stirring occasionally. Spoon into patty shells. Makes 6 servings.

HAM-VEGETABLE STRATA

1 hour cooking time

Advance preparation: Combine one 10½-ounce can condensed cream of mushroom soup and 2 beaten eggs; stir in 1½ cups milk. Cut 4 slices bread into 1-inch cubes. Put *half* of the cubes in 9x9x2-inch baking dish. Top with 1½ cups finely diced fully cooked ham and 1 cup cooked peas; sprinkle with remaining bread cubes. Pour soup mixture over. Cover; chill 6 to 24 hours. Spread 2 slices bread with 1 tablespoon butter; cut into ½-inch cubes. Wrap; chill.
Before serving: Sprinkle buttered bread cubes on casserole. Bake at 325° till set, 50 to 60 minutes; during last few minutes, top with 2 ounces sharp process American cheese, shredded (½ cup). Let stand 10 minutes before serving. Makes 6 servings.

Sprinkle a few chow mein noodles around the edges of Oriental Casserole for a crisp garnish. Then pass the remaining noodles.

ORIENTAL CASSEROLE

1½ hours cooking time

Advance preparation: In skillet cook 1 pound ground beef, ⅓ cup chopped celery, ⅓ cup chopped onion, and ¼ cup chopped green pepper till meat is browned. Drain. Add 1 cup water; bring to boiling.

Combine 2 tablespoons cornstarch, 1 teaspoon sugar, and ¼ teaspoon ground ginger; blend in 2 tablespoons water and ¼ cup soy sauce. Add to beef mixture; cook and stir till thick and bubbly. Stir in one 16-ounce can chop suey vegetables, drained. Break apart one 10-ounce package frozen peas; add to beef mixture. Pour into 2-quart baking dish. Cover; freeze.
Before serving: Bake frozen casserole, covered, at 400° for 1¼ hours. Uncover; bake 15 minutes more. Serve with one 3-ounce can chow mein noodles. Serves 4.

EASY MOUSSAKA
1 hour cooking time

  1 medium, unpeeled eggplant
1½ pounds ground beef
  ½ cup chopped onion
  1 small clove garlic, minced
  1 8-ounce can tomato sauce
  1 tablespoon Worcestershire sauce
     Dash ground nutmeg
  2 cups thinly shredded cabbage
  6 ounces sharp process American
     cheese, shredded (1½ cups)

Advance preparation: Chop eggplant; place in skillet. Add ¼ cup water. Cover and simmer till tender, about 10 to 15 minutes. Pour into a 2-quart baking dish. In same skillet brown the meat, onion, and garlic; drain. Stir in tomato sauce, next 3 ingredients, 1 teaspoon salt, and ¼ teaspoon pepper. Cook, covered, for 10 minutes. Stir in 1 cup of the cheese. Spoon over eggplant. Cover; chill up to 24 hours.
Before serving: Bake, covered, at 350° for 45 minutes. Uncover; top with remaining cheese. Bake 15 minutes more. Serves 6.

TUNA CASSEROLE
55 minutes cooking time

Advance preparation: In saucepan melt 2 tablespoons butter or margarine; blend in 2 tablespoons all-purpose flour and ½ teaspoon onion salt. Stir in one 10½-ounce can condensed cream of celery soup; add 1⅓ cups milk. Cook and stir till thick and bubbly. Add 2 ounces process American cheese, shredded (½ cup); stir till melted. Remove from heat. Stir in one 9¼-ounce can tuna, drained and broken into chunks, and 1 cup cooked peas. Turn into 10x6x1¾-inch baking dish. Cover and freeze.
Before serving: Bake frozen casserole, uncovered, at 425° till bubbly, 40 to 45 minutes; stir occasionally. Halve 1 package refrigerated buttermilk biscuits (6 biscuits); arrange atop *bubbling hot* casserole. Bake till biscuits are golden brown, about 8 to 10 minutes more. Makes 4 servings.

TURKEY CASSEROLE
1¼ hours cooking time

Advance preparation: Cook 1 cup macaroni in boiling, salted water till *almost* tender. Drain; rinse. In saucepan cook ¼ cup chopped green pepper and ¼ cup chopped onion in ¼ cup butter till tender. Blend in ¼ cup all-purpose flour; ½ teaspoon salt; ¼ teaspoon dried marjoram leaves, crushed; and dash pepper. Add 1 cup milk and 1 cup chicken broth. Cook and stir till thick and bubbly. Add 3 ounces process American cheese, shredded (¾ cup); stir to melt. Fold in macaroni and 1½ cups chopped, cooked turkey. Turn into a 1½-quart baking dish. Cover; freeze.
Before serving: Bake frozen casserole, uncovered, at 400° till heated through, 70 minutes. Stir occasionally. Top with 1 ounce process American cheese, shredded (¼ cup); bake 3 to 4 minutes. Serves 6.

CURRIED TURKEY PIE
30 minutes cooking time

  ¼ cup light raisins
1½ cups herb-seasoned stuffing mix
  ¼ cup butter or margarine, melted
  ½ cup milk
  1 10½-ounce can condensed cream
     of celery soup
1½ cups cubed, cooked turkey
  1 cup cooked peas
  1 3-ounce can chopped mushrooms,
     drained
  1 tablespoon finely chopped onion
  1 teaspoon curry powder

Advance preparation: Cover raisins with boiling water; let stand 5 minutes. Drain. Combine stuffing mix, butter, and 2 tablespoons water. Remove ¼ cup crumbs. Wrap; chill. Press remaining crumbs into 9-inch pie plate. Blend milk into soup. Add remaining ingredients and raisins. Turn into crumb shell. Cover; chill up to 24 hours.
Before serving: Sprinkle reserved crumbs atop pie. Bake at 375° till heated through, 25 to 30 minutes. Makes 6 servings.

CHEESE MANICOTTI
50 minutes cooking time

- ¼ cup chopped onion
- 1 clove garlic, crushed
- 2 tablespoons salad oil
- 1 16-ounce can tomatoes, cut up
- 1 8-ounce can tomato sauce
- ⅓ cup water
- 1 teaspoon sugar
- 1 teaspoon dried oregano leaves, crushed
- ¼ teaspoon dried thyme leaves, crushed
- ¼ teaspoon salt
- 1 small bay leaf

• • •

- 12 manicotti shells
- 2 beaten eggs
- 12 ounces fresh ricotta or cream-style cottage cheese (1½ cups)
- 1 8-ounce package shredded mozzarella cheese
- ½ cup grated Parmesan cheese
- ¼ cup snipped parsley
- ¼ teaspoon salt
- Dash pepper

Advance preparation: In a 2-quart saucepan cook onion and garlic in salad oil till tender but not browned. Add tomatoes, tomato sauce, water, sugar, oregano, thyme, the first ¼ teaspoon salt, and bay leaf. Bring to boiling; simmer, uncovered, for 45 minutes. Remove bay leaf.

Meanwhile, cook manicotti shells in boiling, salted water just till tender; drain. Rinse shells in cold water. Combine eggs, ricotta *or* cottage cheese, *half* of the mozzarella, Parmesan cheese, parsley, ¼ teaspoon salt, and pepper. Spoon cheese mixture into manicotti shells.

Pour about *half* of the tomato mixture into a 13½x8¾x1¾-inch baking dish. Arrange stuffed shells in baking dish. Pour remaining sauce over shells. Sprinkle remaining mozzarella cheese over top. Cover with foil and refrigerate up to 24 hours.
Before serving: Bake manicotti, covered, at 350° till hot and bubbly, about 45 to 50 minutes. Makes 6 servings.

Plan to use Blue Cheese-Egg Bake as the main dish for a brunch or lunch, and accompany with bacon, fresh fruit, and rolls.

BLUE CHEESE-EGG BAKE
45 minutes cooking time

Advance preparation: Cut 12 hard-cooked eggs in quarters lengthwise; arrange in 11¾x7½x1¾-inch baking dish. Melt 6 tablespoons butter or margarine. Blend in ⅓ cup all-purpose flour, ½ teaspoon salt, and ⅛ teaspoon pepper. Add 3 cups milk; cook and stir till thick and bubbly. Stir in 2 ounces blue cheese, crumbled (½ cup); ½ cup finely chopped celery; and ¼ cup chopped canned pimiento. Pour sauce over eggs. Cover; refrigerate up to 24 hours.

Toss ⅓ cup finely crushed saltine cracker crumbs with 1 tablespoon melted butter or margarine. Wrap and chill.
Before serving: Bake at 375° for 30 minutes. Sprinkle with crumbs. Bake till heated through, 15 minutes more. Serves 8.

CLASSIC CHEESE STRATA
1 hour cooking time

    8 slices bread
    8 ounces sharp process American
        cheese, sliced
    4 eggs
  2½ cups milk
    1 tablespoon chopped onion
    ½ teaspoon prepared mustard

Advance preparation: Trim crusts from 5 slices bread; cut in half diagonally. Place trimmings and 3 slices *untrimmed* bread in 9x9x2-inch baking dish. Top with cheese. Arrange bread triangles atop cheese. Beat eggs; blend in remaining ingredients, 1½ teaspoons salt, and dash pepper. Pour over bread. Cover; chill 4 to 24 hours.
Before serving: Bake at 325° till knife inserted off-center comes out clean, about 1 hour. Let stand 5 minutes. Serves 6.

CHEESY CRAB STRATA
1¼ hours cooking time

    6 slices bread
      Prepared mustard
    1 7½-ounce can crab meat, drained,
        flaked, and cartilage removed
    ¼ cup thinly sliced celery
    1 tablespoon sliced green onion
    4 ounces sharp process American
        cheese, sliced
    5 eggs
  2½ cups milk

Advance preparation: Lightly spread one side of bread with mustard. Cut slices in thirds. Arrange *half* of the bread, mustard side up, in greased 8x8x2-inch baking dish. Combine crab, celery, and onion; sprinkle over bread in dish. Top with cheese, then remaining bread, mustard side down. Beat eggs; blend in milk and 1 teaspoon salt. Pour over bread; sprinkle with paprika, if desired. Cover; chill 4 to 24 hours.
Before serving: Bake at 325° till knife inserted off-center comes out clean, about 1¼ hours. Let stand 5 minutes. Serves 6.

CHICKEN-RICE SOUP
25 minutes cooking time

    1 4-pound ready-to-cook stewing
        chicken, cut up
    ½ cup finely chopped celery with
        leaves
    2 tablespoons snipped parsley
    2 teaspoons salt
    1 bay leaf
    ½ cup uncooked long-grain rice
    ¼ cup all-purpose flour
    ½ teaspoon paprika
    ½ teaspoon salt
    ⅛ teaspoon pepper
    4 cups milk
    2 tablespoons snipped parsley
    1 cup chicken broth or water
      Salt and pepper

Advance preparation: Place chicken pieces in Dutch oven with water to cover. Add celery, the first 2 tablespoons parsley, 2 teaspoons salt, and bay leaf. Cover; bring to boiling. Simmer over low heat till tender, about 2 hours. Remove chicken from broth; set aside. Discard bay leaf; skim fat from broth. Measure 4 cups broth into saucepan; add rice. Simmer the mixture, covered, till the rice is *barely* tender, about 15 to 20 minutes.

Meanwhile, remove chicken from bones; cut into small pieces. Reserve 1½ cups cut-up chicken (refrigerate remaining chicken in covered container for use in casseroles or sandwiches). Combine flour, paprika, the ½ teaspoon salt, and pepper. Stir in enough of the milk to make a thin paste; add to rice in saucepan along with remaining milk. Stir in the 2 tablespoons parsley. Cook and stir till the mixture is thickened and bubbly. Cool; stir in the 1½ cups chicken. Freeze soup in the two 1-quart freezer containers.
Before serving: Place ½ cup chicken broth *or* water in saucepan; add 1 quart frozen soup. Cook, covered, over medium heat till heated through, 20 to 25 minutes. Add salt and pepper to taste. Repeat with remaining frozen soup and broth as needed. Each quart makes 4 servings.

Ladle piping-hot Beef Chowder—this dish features ground beef, celery, tomatoes, and corn—into individual soup bowls for a colorful, full-flavored, lunchtime or suppertime soup.

BEEF CHOWDER
30 minutes cooking time

- 1½ **pounds ground beef**
- ½ **cup chopped celery**
- ½ **cup chopped onion**
- ⅓ **cup chopped green pepper**
- 2 **10½-ounce cans condensed cream of celery soup**
- 2 **16-ounce cans tomatoes, cut up**
- 1 **17-ounce can whole kernel corn**
- ¼ **cup snipped parsley**

Advance preparation: Cook beef, celery, onion, and green pepper till meat is browned; drain. Add remaining ingredients and ½ teaspoon salt. Simmer, covered, 30 minutes. Pour into containers; freeze.
Before serving: Heat soup, covered, till bubbly, about 30 minutes. Stir often. Add salt to taste. Makes 8 to 10 servings.

LENTIL-HAM SOUP
30 minutes cooking time

Advance preparation: In Dutch oven or large saucepan combine one 16-ounce package lentils; 10 cups water; 1 meaty ham bone (1½ pounds); 1 cup chopped onion; 1 teaspoon salt; ¼ teaspoon dried marjoram leaves, crushed; ⅛ teaspoon pepper; and 1 bay leaf. Cover and simmer for about 1½ hours, stirring occasionally.

Remove bone; cut off meat and dice. Return meat to soup. Add 1½ cups chopped carrot, 1 cup chopped celery, and ¼ cup snipped parsley. Cover and simmer 40 minutes. Divide into meal-sized portions; pour into freezer containers. Freeze.
Before serving: In saucepan heat frozen soup, covered, till heated through, about 30 minutes. Stir occasionally. Season to taste with salt and pepper. Makes 10 servings.

BASIC STEW MIXTURE

Prepare this stew mixture in quantity and freeze. Then, use it to prepare any of the recipes on the following page—

⅓ **cup shortening**
5 **pounds beef stew meat, cut in**
   1½-inch cubes
4 **cups water**
2 **cups chopped onion**
2 **cloves garlic, minced**
1 **teaspoon salt**

Advance preparation: Melt shortening in Dutch oven. Brown a portion of the meat on all sides in the hot shortening. Remove browned meat from Dutch oven; set aside. Repeat browning till all meat is cooked. Return all of the meat to the Dutch oven. Add water, chopped onion, minced garlic, and salt. Bring to boiling. Simmer, covered, till meat is tender, about 1½ to 2 hours. Cover and refrigerate. When cold, skim fat from surface. Pour stew mixture into three 1-quart freezer containers. Seal, label, and freeze. Makes 3 quarts.

Arrange biscuit halves around the edge of Beef Pie for a topping that cooks while the stew bakes. Use either a package of refrigerated buttermilk biscuits or a basic biscuit recipe.

BEEF PIE
10 minutes to assemble
50 minutes cooking time

⅓ recipe frozen Basic Stew Mixture
   (1 quart)
1½ teaspoons salt
1 teaspoon liquid gravy base
1 10-ounce package frozen peas
   and carrots
2 tablespoons snipped parsley
¼ cup all-purpose flour
1 package refrigerated buttermilk
   biscuits (10 biscuits)

Before serving: In saucepan combine stew, ½ cup water, salt, and gravy base. Cover and cook over low heat till thawed, about 20 minutes. Add peas and carrots, and parsley. Cover and simmer till tender, about 5 minutes. Blend flour and ½ cup water; stir into stew. Cook and stir till thick. Pour into a 2-quart baking dish. Cut 7 biscuits in half; place atop *hot* stew. Bake at 450° for 20 to 25 minutes. (Bake remaining biscuits.) Makes 5 or 6 servings.

GERMAN STEW
15 minutes to assemble
35 minutes cooking time

⅓ recipe frozen Basic Stew Mixture
   (1 quart)
¼ cup red wine vinegar
1 teaspoon salt
1 beef bouillon cube, crushed
2 cups shredded cabbage
1 cup shredded, peeled apple
½ cup broken gingersnaps
6 ounces medium noodles, cooked
   and drained
½ teaspoon poppy seed

Before serving: Combine stew, ½ cup water, vinegar, salt, and bouillon cube; thaw, covered, over low heat, about 20 minutes. Add cabbage and apple; cover and simmer for 15 minutes. Add gingersnaps; cook and stir till thick. Toss noodles with poppy seed; serve with stew. Serves 4 or 5.

OLD-FASHIONED STEW
15 minutes to assemble
55 minutes cooking time

⅓ recipe frozen Basic Stew Mixture
   (1 quart)
2 teaspoons salt
1 teaspoon Worcestershire sauce
½ teaspoon paprika
   Dash pepper
1 bay leaf
6 carrots, peeled and quartered
4 potatoes, peeled and quartered
¼ cup all-purpose flour

Before serving: In Dutch oven combine stew, 1½ cups water, salt, Worcestershire sauce, paprika, pepper, and bay leaf. Cover and cook over low heat till thawed, about 20 minutes. Bring to boiling; add carrots and potatoes. Cover and simmer till vegetables are tender, about 35 minutes. Remove bay leaf. Push meat and vegetables to side of pan. Blend ½ cup water with flour. Stir slowly into hot liquid. Cook and stir till thickened and bubbly. Makes 6 servings.

SHORTCUT STEW
10 minutes to assemble
55 minutes cooking time

⅓ recipe frozen Basic Stew Mixture
   (1 quart)
1 8-ounce can stewed tomatoes
1 teaspoon salt
1 teaspoon prepared horseradish
4 carrots, peeled and sliced
1 10-ounce package frozen corn
   and lima beans, thawed
2 tablespoons all-purpose flour

Before serving: In large saucepan combine stew, tomatoes, ½ cup water, salt, and horseradish. Cover and cook over low heat till thawed, 20 to 30 minutes. Add carrots; simmer, covered, 10 minutes. Add corn and lima beans; simmer, covered, till tender, 15 to 20 minutes. Combine flour and ¼ cup water till smooth. Stir into stew; cook and stir till thick and bubbly. Serves 5 or 6.

BASIC OVEN MEATBALLS

Prepare meatballs and freeze. Then use frozen meatballs as a shortcut for preparing the recipes found on these two pages —

    3 beaten eggs
    ¾ cup milk
    3 cups soft bread crumbs
        (about 4½ slices)
    ½ cup finely chopped onion
    2 teaspoons salt
    3 pounds ground beef

Advance preparation: In large mixing bowl combine beaten eggs, milk, bread crumbs, chopped onion, and salt; add meat and mix well. Shape into 6 dozen 1-inch balls. Place *half* of the meatballs in 15½x10½x2¼-inch baking pan. Bake at 375° for 25 to 30 minutes. Remove from pan and cool; repeat with remaining meatballs.

Place cooled meatballs on cookie sheet; freeze firm. Using 24 meatballs per package, wrap meatballs in moisture-vaporproof material. Seal and label. Makes 6 dozen.

SAUERBRATEN MEATBALLS

10 minutes to assemble
20 minutes cooking time

    1 cup pineapple juice
    ¾ cup water
    2 beef bouillon cubes
    ½ cup coarse gingersnap crumbs
    ⅓ cup brown sugar
    ¼ cup raisins
    2 tablespoons lemon juice
    ⅓ recipe frozen Basic Oven
        Meatballs (24)
    Hot cooked rice

Before serving: In saucepan bring pineapple juice, water, and bouillon cubes to boiling. Add gingersnap crumbs, brown sugar, raisins, and lemon juice; cook and stir to dissolve gingersnaps. Add frozen meatballs. Cover and simmer till meatballs are thawed, 15 to 20 minutes; stir occasionally. Serve over hot rice. Makes 4 to 6 servings.

SWEET-SOUR MEATBALLS

10 minutes to assemble
20 minutes cooking time

    1 13¼-ounce can pineapple tidbits
    ½ cup brown sugar
    3 tablespoons cornstarch
    1 cup water
    ⅓ cup vinegar
    1 beef bouillon cube
    1 tablespoon soy sauce
    ⅓ recipe frozen Basic Oven
        Meatballs (24)
    1 green pepper, cut in strips
    1 5-ounce can water chestnuts,
        drained and thinly sliced
    Hot cooked rice

Before serving: Drain pineapple; reserve syrup. In saucepan mix brown sugar and cornstarch. Blend in reserved syrup, water, vinegar, bouillon, and soy sauce. Cook and stir till thick and bubbly. Stir in frozen meatballs, pineapple, green pepper, and water chestnuts. Simmer, covered, till meatballs are thawed, 15 to 20 minutes; stir occasionally. Serve over rice; pass additional soy sauce, if desired. Serves 4 to 6.

MEXICALI BAKE

10 minutes to assemble
35 minutes cooking time

    1 5-ounce jar process cheese spread
    ¼ cup milk
    1 10-ounce can enchilada sauce
    ⅓ recipe frozen Basic Oven
        Meatballs (24)
    1 20-ounce can yellow hominy,
        drained
    2 tablespoons chopped green chilies
    2 cups corn chips, coarsely crushed

Before serving: In oven-going skillet blend cheese spread with milk over low heat; stir in enchilada sauce. Add frozen meatballs, hominy, and chilies. Bring to boiling; stir occasionally. Sprinkle with corn chips; transfer to oven. Bake at 350° for 30 to 35 minutes. Makes 4 to 6 servings.

STROGANOFF MEATBALLS

10 minutes to assemble
25 minutes cooking time

 1 10½-ounce can condensed cream of
   mushroom soup
 ¾ cup milk
 1 3-ounce package cream cheese,
   softened
 2 tablespoons catsup
 ⅛ teaspoon garlic powder
 ⅛ teaspoon ground thyme
 ⅓ recipe frozen Basic Oven
   Meatballs (24)
 1 cup dairy sour cream
 8 ounces medium noodles, cooked
   and drained
   Paprika

Before serving: Combine soup and milk;
add cheese and next 3 ingredients. Cook
and stir over low heat till blended. Stir in
frozen meatballs. Simmer, covered, till
thawed, 15 to 20 minutes; stir occasionally.
Stir in sour cream; heat through, *but do not
boil.* Serve over cooked noodles; sprinkle
with paprika. Makes 4 to 6 servings.

SPANISH MEATBALLS

10 minutes to assemble
30 minutes cooking time

 ½ cup chopped green pepper
 2 tablespoons butter or margarine
 1 28-ounce can tomatoes, cut up
 1 3-ounce can chopped mushrooms
 ¼ cup chili sauce
 1 teaspoon sugar
 1 teaspoon prepared horseradish
 ½ teaspoon salt
 4 ounces uncooked medium noodles
 ⅓ recipe frozen Basic Oven
   Meatballs (24)

Before serving: In skillet cook green pepper
in butter till tender. Add tomatoes, undrained mushrooms, and next 5 ingredients;
mix well. Bring to boiling; stir in frozen
meatballs. Simmer, covered, 25 to 30 minutes; stir frequently. Makes 4 to 6 servings.

SPAGHETTI AND MEATBALLS

15 minutes to assemble
45 minutes cooking time

 2 16-ounce cans tomatoes, cut up
 1 6-ounce can tomato paste
 ¾ cup water
 ½ cup red Burgundy
 ½ cup chopped onion
 ½ cup chopped green pepper
 1 clove garlic, minced
 1 teaspoon sugar
 1 teaspoon salt
 ½ teaspoon chili powder
 ⅓ recipe frozen Basic Oven
   Meatballs (24)
 16 ounces spaghetti, cooked and
   drained
   Grated Parmesan cheese

Before serving: In Dutch oven combine first
10 ingredients; bring to boiling. Add frozen
meatballs. Simmer, uncovered, 45 minutes;
stir occasionally. Serve over spaghetti; pass
Parmesan cheese. Makes 6 to 8 servings.

 TIMELY TIPS

● Meat recipes that require marinating are
naturals for adapting to make-ahead. Like-
wise, meat covered with a sauce lends
itself to advance preparation—the sauce,
which covers the surface of the meat, prevents drying out and preserves the flavor.
● Shortcut the last-minute preparation of
stuffed meats by preparing the stuffing
mixture ahead; cover and refrigerate the
stuffing *separately* from the meat. At serving time, stuff the meat and then bake.
● Meat mixtures that include pasta and/or
vegetables are best if slightly undercooked
during advance preparation. When the
mixture is reheated, the pasta and/or
vegetables finish cooking.
● When cooking frozen meat mixtures, you
can speed up thawing by stirring frequently
—but stir gently to avoid breaking up food.

SALADS READY TO SERVE

SHRIMP-MACARONI SALAD
No final preparation

1 pound shelled shrimp, cooked
1½ cups macaroni shells, cooked and
    drained
4 ounces process American cheese,
    cubed (1 cup)
½ cup chopped celery
¼ cup chopped green pepper
2 tablespoons chopped onion
½ cup mayonnaise or salad dressing
½ cup dairy sour cream
3 tablespoons vinegar
¾ teaspoon salt
    Dash bottled hot pepper sauce

Advance preparation: Cut up shrimp; toss with macaroni, cheese, celery, green pepper, and onion. Blend remaining ingredients; toss with shrimp mixture. Cover; chill.
Before serving: Stir salad. If desired, serve in lettuce-lined bowl and top with green pepper rings. Makes 4 to 6 servings.

CAULIFLOWER-HAM SALAD
No final preparation

1 medium head cauliflower
2 cups fully cooked ham cut in
    strips
½ cup thinly sliced radish
½ cup sliced celery
½ cup mayonnaise or salad dressing
2 tablespoons milk
1 teaspoon sugar
2 teaspoons prepared horseradish

Advance preparation: Separate cauliflower into flowerets; cook, covered, in small amount of boiling, salted water 10 to 15 minutes. Drain thoroughly; cool. Toss cauliflower with ham, radish, and celery. Mix remaining ingredients; toss with ham mixture. Cover; chill thoroughly. Serves 6.

RARE BEEF SALAD
10 minutes final preparation

1 1-pound beef T-bone steak, cut
    1 inch thick
⅔ cup salad oil
1 teaspoon grated lemon peel
⅓ cup lemon juice
1 teaspoon Worcestershire sauce
1 teaspoon prepared mustard
½ teaspoon salt
6 cups torn romaine
4 ounces natural Swiss cheese, cut
    in strips (1 cup)
¼ cup diced green pepper
2 tablespoons sliced green onion
    Salt
    Freshly ground pepper

Advance preparation: Trim excess fat from steak; place meat in shallow baking dish. In screw-top jar combine salad oil, lemon peel, lemon juice, Worcestershire sauce, mustard, and ½ teaspoon salt. Cover and shake vigorously to blend. Pour over steak; cover and marinate overnight in refrigerator (or 4 hours at room temperature).

Next morning, drain meat, reserving marinade for dressing. Broil steak 3 inches from heat to rare doneness, about 5 minutes on each side; cool. Slice steak into thin strips; cover and chill thoroughly.
Before serving: Place torn romaine in salad bowl, arrange steak strips, Swiss cheese, green pepper, and sliced onion over romaine. Toss with some of the reserved marinade; season to taste with salt and freshly ground pepper. Makes 4 servings.

A luncheon special

Richly dressed Shrimp-Macaroni Salad is →
the star attraction at lunch. Accompany with hot rolls and a fresh fruit dessert.

One of the more sophisticated main dish salads, Chicken Salad Supreme features greens topped with lemony chicken cubes.

CHICKEN SALAD SUPREME
10 minutes final preparation

Advance preparation: Dissolve one 3-ounce package lemon-flavored gelatin and ½ teaspoon onion salt in 1 cup boiling water; add ½ cup cold water and 1 tablespoon vinegar. With rotary beater blend in ½ cup dairy sour cream; chill till partially set. Fold in 2 cups finely chopped, cooked chicken; chill in 9x9x2-inch pan till firm.
Before serving: Toss together 6 cups torn iceberg lettuce; 4 cups torn romaine; 1 medium tomato, diced; ⅓ cup sliced pitted ripe olives; and 2 tablespoons Italian salad dressing. Arrange in individual salad bowls. Cut chicken mixture into cubes; arrange atop salads. Makes 8 servings.

CRAB-ARTICHOKE TOSS
5 minutes final preparation

    1 9-ounce package frozen artichokes
    1 3-ounce can sliced mushrooms, drained
    1 small onion, sliced and separated into rings
    ½ cup tarragon vinegar
    ⅓ cup salad oil
    1 tablespoon sugar
    2 tablespoons chopped canned pimiento
    1 tablespoon snipped parsley
    1 small clove garlic, crushed
    ¼ teaspoon dried oregano leaves, crushed
    6 cups torn lettuce
    1 7½-ounce can crab meat, chilled, drained, flaked, and cartilage removed
    2 hard-cooked eggs, sliced

Advance preparation: Cook artichokes following package directions; drain. In deep bowl combine artichokes, mushrooms, and onion. Mix vinegar, next 6 ingredients, and ¼ cup water; pour over artichoke mixture. Cover. Chill overnight; stir occasionally.
Before serving: Combine lettuce and crab; toss with undrained artichoke mixture. Garnish with egg slices. Makes 6 servings.

CELERY SLAW
No final preparation

    1 tablespoon sugar
    ½ teaspoon salt
    ½ teaspoon paprika
    Dash pepper
    2 tablespoons salad oil
    1 tablespoon wine vinegar
    ⅓ cup dairy sour cream
    3 cups thinly sliced celery
    ½ cup shredded carrot

Advance preparation: Combine first 6 ingredients; slowly stir into sour cream. Mix celery and carrot; toss lightly with sour cream mixture. Cover; chill. Serves 6 to 8.

POTATO SALAD ROLL
5 minutes final preparation

3 medium potatoes
⅓ cup mayonnaise
1 teaspoon salt
½ teaspoon paprika
3 hard-cooked eggs, finely chopped
½ cup diced celery
2 tablespoons finely chopped onion
1 cup cream-style cottage cheese
2 tablespoons finely chopped green
    pepper
2 tablespoons diced canned pimiento
2 tablespoons mayonnaise

Advance preparation: Peel, cook, and mash potatoes. *Do not add liquid.* Combine potatoes (3 cups) and next 3 ingredients; stir in eggs, celery, and onion. Chill.

Pat into 12x9-inch rectangle on foil. Drain cottage cheese; combine with remaining ingredients. Spread on rectangle to within 1 inch of edges. Roll up jelly-roll fashion, beginning with narrow side; chill.
Before serving: Cut well-chilled potato roll into slices. Makes 6 servings.

CHEESY POTATO SALAD
No final preparation

¼ cup finely chopped onion
1 tablespoon salad oil
1 tablespoon all-purpose flour
1 tablespoon sugar
¼ teaspoon dry mustard
3 tablespoons vinegar
2½ cups, diced, cooked potatoes
½ cup chopped celery
2 tablespoons chopped green pepper
2 ounces process American cheese,
    shredded (½ cup)

Advance preparation: Cook onion in oil till tender. Blend in flour, sugar, 1 teaspoon salt, and mustard. Mix ¼ cup water and vinegar; add to mixture. Cook and stir till thick and bubbly; cook and stir 2 minutes more. Mix remaining ingredients; toss with hot mixture. Cover; chill. Serves 4.

FAVORITE POTATO SALAD
No final preparation

4 medium potatoes
    Few celery leaves
1 bay leaf
1 cup sliced celery
⅓ cup chopped green pepper
⅓ cup finely chopped onion
3 hard-cooked eggs, chopped
2 tablespoons snipped parsley
1 cup mayonnaise or salad dressing
1 teaspoon prepared mustard

Advance preparation: In saucepan combine first 3 ingredients and 1 teaspoon salt; add water to almost cover. Cook, covered, till tender, 30 to 40 minutes; drain, peel, and cube potatoes. Combine potatoes, sliced celery, and next 4 ingredients. Blend mayonnaise, 1 teaspoon salt, and mustard; toss with potato mixture. If desired, top with paprika. Cover; chill. Makes 8 servings.

TOMATO-CUCUMBER SALAD
5 minutes final preparation

2 medium tomatoes, sliced
1 medium cucumber, peeled and
    thinly sliced
½ medium onion, thinly sliced and
    separated into rings
½ cup salad oil
¼ cup white wine vinegar
1 teaspoon salt
1 teaspoon dried basil leaves,
    crushed
1 teaspoon dried tarragon leaves,
    crushed
⅛ teaspoon pepper
    Shredded lettuce

Advance preparation: Layer tomato, cucumber, and onion in shallow glass dish. Mix oil with next 5 ingredients; beat with rotary or electric beater. Pour over vegetables; chill, covered, 5 to 6 hours.
Before serving: Drain vegetables; reserve marinade. Arrange vegetables on lettuce; pass reserved marinade. Makes 6 servings.

ANCHOVY-BEAN TOSS
10 minutes final preparation

- 1 16-ounce can whole green beans, drained
- 1 medium onion, sliced and separated into rings
- ⅓ cup pitted ripe olives, sliced
- 1 2-ounce can anchovy fillets, drained and chopped
- 2 tablespoons snipped parsley
- 1 clove garlic, minced
- 1 cup Italian salad dressing
- 1 large head Boston lettuce, torn in bite-sized pieces (6 cups)
- 3 tomatoes, cut in wedges
- 3 hard-cooked eggs, sliced

Advance preparation: Combine first 6 ingredients; toss with salad dressing. Cover bean mixture and chill thoroughly.
Before serving: Drain bean mixture, reserving dressing. In salad bowl combine lettuce, bean mixture, and desired amount of reserved dressing; toss lightly. Top with tomato wedges and egg slices. Serves 8.

ENSALADA CONCHITA
No final preparation

- 1 12-ounce can vacuum-packed corn with peppers
- 1 8½-ounce can peas
- 1 8½-ounce can green lima beans
- 1 8-ounce can cut green beans
- 1 cup diced celery
- 2 hard-cooked eggs, chopped
- ¼ cup mayonnaise or salad dressing
- ¼ cup dairy sour cream
- 1 teaspoon prepared mustard
- 1 teaspoon Worcestershire sauce
- ½ teaspoon onion salt
- ½ teaspoon curry powder
  Dash hot pepper sauce

Advance preparation: Drain canned vegetables; toss with celery and eggs. Blend together remaining ingredients; toss with vegetable mixture. Cover; chill thoroughly, stirring once or twice. Makes 10 servings.

SAVORY BEAN SALAD
No final preparation

- 1 16-ounce can cut green beans
- 2 tomatoes, cut in eighths
- 2 tablespoons chopped onion
- ⅓ cup clear French salad dressing with herbs and spices
- ½ cup dairy sour cream
- 1 teaspoon prepared horseradish
- ½ teaspoon seasoned salt
- ½ teaspoon dry mustard

Advance preparation: Drain beans; add tomatoes, onion, and salad dressing, stirring to coat. Cover; chill several hours, stirring once or twice. Combine sour cream, horseradish, salt, and mustard; toss with bean mixture. Cover; chill thoroughly.
Before serving: If desired, spoon salad into lettuce cups. Makes 6 servings.

24-HOUR SALAD
No final preparation

- 1 20½-ounce can pineapple tidbits
- 3 egg yolks
- 2 tablespoons sugar
- 2 tablespoons vinegar
- 1 tablespoon butter or margarine
  Dash salt
- 1 16-ounce can pitted light sweet cherries, drained
- 3 oranges, peeled, diced, and drained
- 2 cups miniature marshmallows
- 1 cup whipping cream

Advance preparation: Drain pineapple; reserve 2 tablespoons syrup. In top of double boiler beat egg yolks slightly; add reserved syrup, sugar, vinegar, butter, and salt. Cook and stir over hot water till sauce thickens slightly and barely coats a spoon, about 12 minutes. Cool to room temperature. Combine fruits and marshmallows; mix gently with sauce. Whip cream; fold into salad. Cover; chill 24 hours.
Before serving: If desired, top with orange sections and mint leaves. Serves 6 to 8.

CRANBERRY FLUFF
No final preparation

   2 cups fresh cranberries, ground
   3 cups miniature marshmallows
   ¾ cup sugar
   • • •
   2 cups diced, unpeeled, tart apple
   ½ cup seedless green grapes, halved
   ½ cup broken walnuts
   ¼ teaspoon salt
   1 cup whipping cream

Advance preparation: Combine cranberries, marshmallows, and sugar. Cover and chill overnight. Stir in diced apple, grapes, walnuts, and salt. Whip cream; gently fold cream into fruit mixture. Cover and chill thoroughly. Makes 8 to 10 servings.

FLUFFY ORANGE SALAD
No final preparation

   1 3-ounce package cream cheese
   1 5-ounce jar Neufchâtel cheese
      spread with pimiento
   1 16-ounce can sliced peaches
   1 13½-ounce can pineapple tidbits
   1 11-ounce can mandarin orange
      sections
   1 cup miniature marshmallows
   1 cup whipping cream

Advance preparation: Soften cream cheese; beat with cheese spread. Drain fruits, reserving ¼ cup *peach* syrup. Beat reserved syrup into cheese. Cut up peaches; fold fruits and marshmallows into cheese. Whip cream; fold in. Cover; chill. Serves 8.

A classic make-ahead, 24-Hour Salad blends the delicate flavors of pineapple, light sweet cherries, and oranges in a rich, custard sauce. Serve the fruit salad with freshly baked date muffins.

CHEESE SOUFFLÉ SALAD
No final preparation

1 3-ounce package lemon-flavored
    gelatin
1 cup boiling water
⅓ cup cold water
½ cup mayonnaise or salad dressing
2 tablespoons lemon juice
¾ teaspoon salt
3 or 4 drops bottled hot pepper
    sauce
2 ounces sharp process American
    cheese, shredded (½ cup)
2 hard-cooked eggs, coarsely
    chopped
½ cup chopped celery
2 tablespoons chopped green pepper
2 tablespoons chopped canned
    pimiento
½ teaspoon grated onion

Advance preparation: Dissolve gelatin in boiling water. Add cold water, mayonnaise, lemon juice, salt, and hot pepper sauce. Blend well with electric mixer or rotary beater; chill till partially set.

Beat mixture till fluffy. Fold in remaining ingredients. Pour mixture into a 4½-cup mold; chill till firm. Makes 6 servings.

LEMON-PINEAPPLE RING
5 minutes final preparation

2 3-ounce packages lemon-flavored
    gelatin
1 pint lemon sherbet
1 8¾-ounce can crushed pineapple
1½ cups small curd cream-style
    cottage cheese

Advance preparation: Dissolve gelatin in 2 cups boiling water. Add sherbet, a spoonful at a time, stirring till melted. Stir in *undrained* pineapple. Chill till partially set. Fold in cottage cheese; pour into 6½-cup ring mold. Chill till firm.
Before serving: Unmold salad. If desired, fill center of ring with fresh raspberries and strawberry halves. Makes 10 servings.

BERRY-WINE SALAD
5 minutes final preparation

1 6-ounce or two 3-ounce packages
    raspberry-flavored gelatin
2 cups boiling water
1 16-ounce can whole cranberry
    sauce
1 8¾-ounce can crushed pineapple
½ cup Burgundy
⅓ cup chopped walnuts
    • • •
1 2-ounce envelope dessert topping
    mix
1 8-ounce package cream cheese,
    softened
1 teaspoon grated orange peel
    Lettuce

Advance preparation: Dissolve gelatin in boiling water. Stir in cranberry sauce, undrained pineapple, and Burgundy. Chill till partially set. Stir in walnuts; pour into 6½-cup mold. Chill till firm.

Meanwhile, prepare dessert topping mix according to package directions. Beat in cream cheese; fold in peel. Cover; chill.
Before serving: Unmold salad on lettuce-lined platter. Serve with well-chilled dressing. Makes 10 to 12 servings.

ORANGE-PORT MOLD
No final preparation

2 3-ounce packages black cherry-
    flavored gelatin
1½ cups boiling water
3 oranges
1 cup port wine
1 cup orange juice

Advance preparation: Dissolve gelatin in boiling water. Peel and section oranges, reserving juice; cut up pulp. Add water to reserved juice to make ½ cup. Stir into dissolved gelatin along with wine and the additional 1 cup orange juice. Chill till mixture is partially set. Fold in cut-up oranges; pour into 6½-cup ring mold. Chill till firm. Makes 8 to 10 servings.

COOL CUCUMBER MOLDS
No final preparation

  1 3-ounce package lime-flavored
      gelatin
  1 cup boiling water
  1 tablespoon vinegar
  1 teaspoon onion juice
  1 large cucumber
  1 8-ounce carton plain yogurt

Advance preparation: Dissolve lime-flavored gelatin in boiling water. Add vinegar and onion juice. Chill till partially set.

Meanwhile, halve unpeeled cucumber lengthwise and remove seeds; chop cucumber to make 1 cup. Blend yogurt into partially set gelatin mixture; stir in chopped cucumber. Pour salad mixture into 6 or 7 individual salad molds. Chill salad till firm. Makes 6 or 7 servings.

PEACH-BERRY MARBLE
No final preparation

  1 3-ounce package raspberry-flavored
      gelatin
  2 cups fresh raspberries
            • • •
  1 envelope unflavored gelatin
      (1 tablespoon)
  2 tablespoons lemon juice
  1 2-ounce envelope dessert topping
      mix
  2 3-ounce packages cream cheese,
      softened
  2 cups diced, peeled, fresh peaches

Advance preparation: Dissolve raspberry gelatin in 1 cup boiling water; stir in ½ cup cold water. Chill till partially set. Fold in berries. Soften unflavored gelatin in ⅔ cup cold water; dissolve over hot water. Stir in lemon juice; cool.

Prepare topping mix following package directions; beat in cheese. Fold in unflavored gelatin. Chill till partially set; fold in peaches. Layer berry and peach mixtures in 7½-cup mold; swirl with spoon to marble. Chill overnight. Serves 10.

LIME-APPLESAUCE MOLD
No final preparation

As pictured on the front cover—

Advance preparation: In saucepan combine one 16-ounce can applesauce and one 3-ounce package lime-flavored gelatin. Cook and stir till gelatin dissolves; cool to room temperature. Gently stir in one 7-ounce bottle lemon-lime carbonated beverage (about 1 cup). Turn into a 3½-cup mold. Chill till firm. Makes 6 servings.

LEMON-WALDORF MOLD
No final preparation

Lemon adds zest to a classic salad—

  1 3-ounce package lemon-flavored
      gelatin
  1 cup buttermilk
  1 apple, cored and chopped (1 cup)
  ¼ cup chopped celery
  ¼ cup chopped walnuts

Advance preparation: Dissolve gelatin in 1 cup boiling water; stir in buttermilk. Fold in remaining ingredients; turn into 3½-cup mold. Chill till firm. Serves 4 to 6.

PEAR-MINT MOLD
No final preparation

  1 3-ounce package lime-flavored
      gelatin
  1 8¾-ounce can pineapple tidbits
  3 tablespoons crème de menthe syrup
  ½ cup dairy sour cream
  1 cup diced, peeled, fresh pear

Advance preparation: Dissolve gelatin in 1 cup boiling water. Drain pineapple; reserve syrup. Add crème de menthe syrup to reserved syrup; add water to equal ¾ cup. Stir into gelatin. Beat into sour cream with rotary beater. Chill till partially set. Whip till light; fold in fruits. Turn into 4½-cup mold. Chill till firm. Makes 4 servings.

CRANBERRY FREEZE
5 minutes final preparation

1 16-ounce can whole cranberry
  sauce
1 8¾-ounce can crushed pineapple,
  drained

· · ·

1 cup dairy sour cream
¼ cup sifted confectioners' sugar

· · ·

3 pineapple rings, well drained
  Lettuce

Advance preparation: In medium bowl combine cranberry sauce and crushed pineapple. In small bowl stir together dairy sour cream and sifted confectioners' sugar; add to fruit mixture, mixing ingredients well. Line a 3-cup refrigerator tray with foil; pour in fruit mixture. Freeze firm.
Before serving: Lift frozen salad and foil from pan; let stand a few minutes at room temperature. Remove foil; cut salad into 6 wedges. Cut well-drained pineapple rings in half; arrange each *half* atop a cranberry wedge. Serve the salad on a lettuce-lined platter. Makes 6 servings.

Simple to make and scrumptious to eat, cool and colorful Cranberry Freeze is a welcome salad treat for guests and hostess alike.

STRAWBERRY FROSTIES
No final preparation

1 8-ounce carton strawberry-flavored
  yogurt
¼ cup sugar
1 8¾-ounce can fruit cocktail,
  well drained
2 tablespoons chopped pecans

Advance preparation: Combine yogurt and sugar; stir in fruit cocktail and pecans. Line muffin pan with paper bake cups; spoon in salad. Freeze firm, at least 2 hours.
Before serving: Let salads stand at room temperature a few minutes; remove papers before serving. Makes 6 servings.

SPICY PEACH FREEZE
No final preparation

1 29-ounce can peach slices
½ of one 6-ounce can frozen orange
  juice concentrate, thawed
  (⅓ cup)
4 inches stick cinnamon
5 whole cloves

· · ·

2 3-ounce packages cream cheese,
  softened
3 tablespoons mayonnaise
1 cup whipping cream

Advance preparation: Drain peaches, reserving syrup. Chop peaches; set aside. In small saucepan combine reserved syrup, orange juice concentrate, cinnamon, and cloves; bring to boiling. Reduce heat; simmer, uncovered, for 5 minutes. Remove from heat; cool. Remove spices and discard.
  Beat cream cheese with mayonnaise; gradually stir in juice mixture. Add peaches; mix well. Whip cream; fold into fruit mixture. Line 9x9x2-inch baking pan with foil; turn salad into pan. Cover; freeze.
Before serving: Lift frozen salad and foil from pan; let stand at room temperature 10 to 15 minutes before serving. Remove foil. Cut into serving pieces; serve on lettuce, if desired. Makes 8 to 10 servings.

FROZEN FRUIT CUBES
5 minutes final preparation

1 large banana, diced (1 cup)
1 8¾-ounce can crushed pineapple, drained
3 tablespoons slivered almonds, toasted
½ cup mayonnaise or salad dressing
½ cup whipping cream

Advance preparation: Combine first 3 ingredients; fold in mayonnaise. Whip cream; fold into fruit mixture. Turn into 3-cup refrigerator tray; freeze 4 to 5 hours.
Before serving: Remove salad from freezer; let stand at room temperature for 10 minutes. Cut salad into cubes. If desired, serve on lettuce and top with additional toasted, slivered almonds. Makes 6 servings.

FROSTY FRUIT MOLDS
No final preparation

1 8-ounce package cream cheese, softened
¼ cup mayonnaise or salad dressing
¼ cup sifted confectioners' sugar
2 tablespoons lemon juice
½ teaspoon vanilla
• • •
1 10-ounce package frozen blueberries, thawed and drained
1 10-ounce package frozen peaches, thawed, drained, and cut up
1 8¾-ounce can pineapple tidbits, drained
1 cup miniature marshmallows
1 cup whipping cream

Advance preparation: Combine cream cheese, mayonnaise, confectioners' sugar, lemon juice, and vanilla; beat smooth. Fold in fruits and marshmallows. Whip cream; fold into fruit mixture. Turn into 12 individual molds or one 6½-cup mold; freeze.
Before serving: Allow salads to stand at room temperature, 10 to 15 minutes for individual molds and 20 to 30 minutes for 6½ cup mold. Unmold. Makes 12 servings.

FROZEN AMBROSIA
5 minutes final preparation

1 3-ounce package cream cheese, softened
½ cup sifted confectioners' sugar
1 cup dairy sour cream
½ of one 6-ounce can frozen orange juice concentrate, thawed (⅓ cup)
½ cup whipping cream
1 16-ounce can fruit cocktail, drained
1 11-ounce can mandarin orange sections, drained
• • •
Lettuce leaves
¼ cup flaked coconut, toasted

Advance preparation: Beat cream cheese with confectioners' sugar; gradually beat in sour cream and concentrate. Whip cream; fold into cheese mixture. Stir in fruit cocktail and orange sections. Spread in 9x9x2-inch baking pan. Freeze till firm.
Before serving: Let frozen salad stand at room temperature 10 minutes. Cut into serving pieces. Serve on lettuce leaves; sprinkle with coconut. Serves 8 to 10.

TIMELY TIPS

• Unless salad ingredients need to marinate in the dressing mixture, cover and chill salad dressing separately; lightly toss dressing with salad just before serving.
• To speed up the preparation of tossed salads, clean salad ingredients and chop firm vegetables, such as celery, carrots, and green pepper, early in the day. Wrap and chill vegetables till serving time.
• Keep frozen salads on hand for quick menus. Freeze salad mixtures in paper bake cups; at mealtime, remove number of salads needed from freezer.
• Many salads, such as potato, improve in flavor during storage, so prepare a day or two ahead, even if time isn't a factor.

VEGETABLES AND RELISHES ALWAYS ON CALL

FRENCH ONION CASSEROLE

40 minutes cooking time

    4 medium onions, sliced
    3 tablespoons butter
    2 tablespoons all-purpose flour
    1 cup beef bouillon
    ¼ cup dry sherry
    1½ cups plain croutons
    2 tablespoons butter, melted
    ¼ cup shredded process Swiss cheese
    2 tablespoons grated Parmesan
        cheese

Advance preparation: Cook onions in 3 tablespoons butter till tender. Blend in flour and dash pepper. Add bouillon and sherry; cook and stir till thick and bubbly. Turn into 1-quart casserole. Cover; chill. Toss croutons with melted butter; chill.
Before serving: Bake casserole, covered, at 350° for 30 minutes. Sprinkle with croutons, then cheeses. Bake, uncovered, 5 to 10 minutes more. Makes 4 to 6 servings.

LIMA CASSEROLE

40 minutes cooking time

Advance preparation: Rinse 8 ounces large dry limas (1 cup); place in large saucepan with 3 cups water. Bring to boiling; cover and simmer 2 minutes. Remove from heat; let stand 1 hour. Do not drain. Return to heat; simmer, covered, 1 hour.

Add 2 ounces process American cheese, shredded (½ cup); ⅓ cup chopped onion; ½ teaspoon salt; ¼ teaspoon ground sage; and dash pepper. Mix. Turn into 1-quart casserole. Partially cook 3 slices bacon; drain. Crumble over beans. Cover; chill.
Before serving: Bake casserole, covered, at 375° for 30 minutes. Uncover; bake 10 minutes longer. Makes 3 or 4 servings.

BROCCOLI-ONION DELUXE

1 hour cooking time

    1 pound fresh broccoli or
        two 10-ounce packages frozen
        cut broccoli
    2 cups frozen whole small onions or
        3 medium onions, quartered
            • • •
    4 tablespoons butter or margarine
    2 tablespoons all-purpose flour
    1 cup milk
    1 3-ounce package cream cheese
    2 ounces sharp process American
        cheese, shredded (½ cup)
    1 cup soft bread crumbs

Advance preparation: Slit fresh broccoli spears lengthwise; cut into 1-inch pieces. Cook in boiling, salted water till tender. (Or cook frozen broccoli according to package directions.) Drain. Cook onions in boiling, salted water till tender; drain.

In saucepan melt *2 tablespoons* of the butter; blend in flour, ¼ teaspoon salt, and dash pepper. Add milk; cook and stir till thick and bubbly. Reduce heat; blend in cream cheese till smooth. Place vegetables in a 1½-quart casserole. Pour sauce over; mix lightly. Top with process cheese; cover and chill. Melt remaining butter; toss with crumbs. Cover; chill.
Before serving: Bake casserole, covered, at 350° for 30 minutes. Sprinkle crumbs around edge; bake, uncovered, till heated through, about 30 minutes more. Serves 6.

Versatile vegetables

Dramatic in both its color and flavor, → Broccoli-Onion Deluxe is assembled early in the day, then baked just before serving.

Bursting with a rich and tangy sour cream flavor, Frozen Baked Potatoes are prepared in advance and frozen until ready to use.

CREAMY POTATO BAKE
50 minutes cooking time

- ¾ cup milk
- 2 3-ounce packages cream cheese, softened
- 1 tablespoon snipped chives
- ½ teaspoon instant minced onion
- 4 cups cubed, peeled, cooked potatoes (4 medium)

Advance preparation: Over low heat gradually blend milk into cream cheese till smooth. Stir in chives, onion, and 1 teaspoon salt. Add potatoes; stir gently. Turn into a 1½-quart casserole. Cover; chill.
Before serving: Bake, covered, at 375° for 30 minutes. Stir; bake, uncovered, 20 minutes longer. Stir again; sprinkle with paprika, if desired. Serves 6 to 8.

FROZEN BAKED POTATOES
40 minutes cooking time

Advance preparation: Scrub 5 medium baking potatoes; bake at 425° till tender, 50 to 60 minutes. With electric mixer blend together ⅔ cup milk; one 2½-ounce envelope sour cream sauce mix; ¾ teaspoon salt; ¼ teaspoon ground cumin seed (optional); and dash pepper. Let stand 10 minutes.

Cut thin, lengthwise slice from each potato; discard. Scoop out centers; add to sauce mixture with 2 tablespoons butter. Beat till fluffy; add more milk, if needed. Spoon into potato shells; sprinkle with paprika. Freeze, covered, up to 2 weeks.
Before serving: Heat potatoes, uncovered, at 375° till hot, about 40 minutes. Meanwhile, fry 5 slices bacon; drain. Form into curls; secure with wooden picks. Top each potato with bacon curl. Makes 5 servings.

CELERY-CHEESE BAKE
40 minutes cooking time

- 4 cups sliced celery, cut ½ inch thick
- ¼ cup butter
- 2 tablespoons all-purpose flour
- ¾ cup milk
- 1 3-ounce can chopped mushrooms
- 2 tablespoons chopped green pepper
- 2 tablespoons chopped canned pimiento
- 4 ounces sharp process American cheese, shredded (1 cup)
- 1 cup soft bread crumbs
- 2 tablespoons butter, melted

Advance preparation: Cook celery in ¼ cup butter till tender, 5 to 10 minutes. Stir in flour and ¼ teaspoon salt. Add milk; cook and stir till thick and bubbly. Drain mushrooms. Add mushrooms and next 3 ingredients to sauce; stir till cheese melts. Pour into 1-quart casserole. Cover; chill. Toss crumbs with melted butter; chill.
Before serving: Bake, covered, at 375° for 20 minutes; stir. Sprinkle with crumbs. Bake, uncovered, 20 minutes. Serves 6.

CORN-MUSHROOM BAKE
50 minutes cooking time

¼ cup all-purpose flour
1 16-ounce can cream-style corn
1 3-ounce package cream cheese,
  cut in cubes
½ teaspoon onion salt
1 16-ounce can whole kernel corn
1 6-ounce can sliced mushrooms
2 ounces process Swiss cheese,
  shredded (½ cup)
1½ cups soft bread crumbs
3 tablespoons butter, melted

Advance preparation: Stir flour into cream-style corn. Add cream cheese and onion salt; heat and stir till cheese melts. Drain whole kernel corn and mushrooms; stir into hot mixture with Swiss cheese. Pour into 1½-quart casserole; cover and chill. Toss crumbs with butter; cover and chill.
Before serving: Bake casserole, covered, at 400° for 30 minutes. Top with crumbs; bake, uncovered, 20 minutes. Serves 6 to 8.

CORN-TOMATO SCALLOP
50 minutes cooking time

1 well-beaten egg
1 17-ounce can cream-style corn
¾ cup milk
1½ cups finely crushed saltine
  crackers (about 42)
¼ cup finely chopped onion
2 tablespoons snipped parsley
1 tablespoon sugar
3 tomatoes, peeled and sliced
1 tablespoon butter, melted

Advance preparation: Combine egg, corn, and milk. Add 1 cup of the cracker crumbs, onion, parsley, sugar, and 1 teaspoon salt; mix well. Layer *half* of the tomato slices in 8-inch round baking dish; top with *half* of the corn mixture. Repeat. Cover; chill. Toss remaining crumbs with butter; chill.
Before serving: Sprinkle casserole with buttered crumbs. Bake, uncovered, at 375° till set, 45 to 50 minutes. Serves 8.

COMPANY SQUASH
50 minutes cooking time

1 pound yellow summer squash
1 medium onion
2 tablespoons butter
3 tablespoons all-purpose flour
1 cup milk
4 ounces sharp process American
  cheese, shredded (1 cup)
1 3-ounce can sliced mushrooms,
  drained
½ cup soft bread crumbs
¼ cup chopped pecans
1 tablespoon butter, melted

Advance preparation: Cut squash and onion into ¼-inch slices. Cook in boiling, salted water till tender; drain. In saucepan melt 2 tablespoons butter; blend in flour. Add milk; cook and stir till thick and bubbly. Add cheese and mushrooms; stir till cheese melts. Arrange *half* of the vegetables in 1½-quart casserole; cover with *half* of the sauce. Repeat. Cover and chill. Toss remaining ingredients; cover and chill.
Before serving: Bake squash, covered, at 350° for 25 minutes. Sprinkle with pecan mixture; bake, uncovered, 20 to 25 minutes longer. Makes 6 to 8 servings.

ASPARAGUS CASSEROLE
45 minutes cooking time

Advance preparation: In saucepan cook ½ cup celery in ¼ cup butter; blend in ¼ cup all-purpose flour, ¼ teaspoon salt, and dash pepper. Add 1 cup milk, ¾ cup water, and 1 chicken bouillon cube; cook and stir till thick and bubbly. Stir in one 3-ounce can chopped mushrooms, drained.
  Cook two 10-ounce packages frozen cut asparagus following package directions; drain. Place in 10x6x1¾-inch baking dish; top with 3 hard-cooked eggs, sliced. Pour sauce over. Cover; chill up to 6 hours.
Before serving: Bake casserole, covered, at 375° for 30 minutes. Sprinkle with ½ cup finely crushed round cheese crackers; bake, uncovered, 15 minutes more. Serves 6.

CRAN-ORANGE RELISH
No final preparation

    1 pound fresh cranberries
    2 cups sugar
    ½ cup water
    1 teaspoon grated orange peel
    ½ cup orange juice
    ½ cup slivered almonds

Advance preparation: In saucepan combine fresh cranberries, sugar, water, grated orange peel, and orange juice. Cook, uncovered, till cranberry skins pop, about 10 minutes; stir mixture once or twice.

Remove from heat; stir slivered almonds into cranberry mixture. Cool at room temperature. Store relish in covered container in refrigerator. Makes about 4 cups.

SPICED PEACHES
No final preparation

    1 29-ounce can peach halves
    ¼ cup sugar
    1 tablespoon vinegar
    6 inches stick cinnamon
    ½ teaspoon whole cloves
    ¼ cup brandy (optional)

Advance preparation: Drain peach halves, reserving syrup; set peaches aside. In small saucepan combine reserved peach syrup, sugar, vinegar, stick cinnamon, and whole cloves. Simmer syrup mixture, uncovered, for 5 minutes. Add peach halves; heat through. Cool. Stir in brandy. Store peaches in covered container in refrigerator at least 48 hours before serving.

Sassy vegetable relishes, such as Corn Relish, Tomato Relish, and Pickled Mushrooms, improve in flavor when allowed to marinate in the refrigerator for a few days before serving.

CORN RELISH
No final preparation

   1 10-ounce package frozen corn
½ cup sugar
   1 tablespoon cornstarch
½ cup vinegar
⅓ cup cold water
   2 tablespoons finely chopped celery
   2 tablespoons minced green pepper
   2 tablespoons minced canned
      pimiento
   1 tablespoon minced onion
   1 teaspoon ground turmeric
½ teaspoon dry mustard

Advance preparation: Cook corn according to package directions; drain. In saucepan mix sugar and cornstarch; stir in vinegar and water. Add corn, celery, green pepper, pimiento, onion, turmeric, and dry mustard. Cook and stir till thickened and bubbly; cook and stir 3 to 4 minutes more. Cover; chill thoroughly. Makes 2 cups.

PICKLED MUSHROOMS
No final preparation

⅓ cup dry white wine
⅓ cup white wine vinegar
⅓ cup salad oil
   1 small onion, thinly sliced and
      separated into rings
   2 tablespoons snipped parsley
   1 small clove garlic, crushed
   1 bay leaf
   1 teaspoon salt
¼ teaspoon dried thyme leaves,
      crushed
   Dash freshly ground pepper
   2 6-ounce cans whole mushrooms,
      drained

Advance preparation: In saucepan combine all ingredients except mushrooms; bring to boiling. Add mushrooms; return mixture to boiling. Simmer, uncovered, for 10 minutes. Cool; chill in covered container at least 24 hours before serving. Store in refrigerator up to 2 weeks. Makes 2 cups.

TOMATO RELISH
No final preparation

   5 medium tomatoes
   1 medium green pepper, finely chopped
   1 medium onion, finely chopped
   1 stalk celery, finely chopped
   1 tablespoon prepared horseradish
   2 teaspoons salt
      • • •
¾ cup vinegar
½ cup sugar
   1 teaspoon mustard seed
⅛ teaspoon ground cloves
   Dash pepper

Advance preparation: Peel tomatoes and remove seeds; chop. (Should have about 2¾ cups.) Combine tomatoes, chopped vegetables, horseradish, and salt. Cover; let stand for 2 hours at room temperature.

   Thoroughly drain vegetables; stir vinegar, sugar, mustard seed, cloves, and pepper into tomato mixture. Chill in covered container at least 24 hours before serving. Keeps up to 4 days. Makes 2½ cups.

 TIMELY TIPS

● Vegetables used in a make-ahead casserole are best if slightly undercooked during the advance preparation. The vegetables finish cooking when the casserole is heated.
● Keep a supply of chopped onion in a tightly covered container in the refrigerator or freezer to speed the preparation of favorite main dishes, casseroles, and salads.
● Many vegetable dishes are prepared with cheese. To save time, shred cheese in a quantity that will be used in a few days; cover and store cheese in the refrigerator.
● To avoid a soggy topping, wrap and chill buttered bread crumbs separately from casserole mixtures prepared in advance.
● Vegetable and fruit relishes generally improve in flavor when allowed to marinate in the refrigerator for a few days.

54

LAST-MINUTE BREADS

ORANGE COFFEE CAKE
35 minutes cooking time

2 envelopes active dry yeast
¼ cup granulated sugar
2 eggs
½ cup dairy sour cream
6 tablespoons butter
1 teaspoon salt
3¾ cups sifted all-purpose flour
⅔ cup granulated sugar
1 cup flaked coconut, toasted
2 tablespoons shredded orange peel
2 tablespoons butter, melted
1 cup sifted confectioners' sugar
3 to 4 teaspoons orange juice

Advance preparation: Soften yeast in ½ cup warm water. In mixing bowl combine ¼ cup granulated sugar and next 4 ingredients; stir in yeast. Gradually add enough flour to form a moderately stiff dough, beating well. Cover; let rise in warm place till double, about 45 minutes. Mix ⅔ cup granulated sugar, coconut, and orange peel.

Knead dough a few strokes on well-floured surface. Roll *half* of the dough to 12x8-inch rectangle. Brush with 1 *tablespoon* of the melted butter; sprinkle with ½ *cup* of the coconut mixture. Roll up, starting with long side. Cut into 12 1-inch slices. Place rolls, cut side down, in greased 9x1½-inch round baking pan. Repeat with remaining dough, butter, and ½ *cup* of the coconut mixture. Let rise in warm place till light, 30 to 45 minutes.

Sprinkle rolls with remaining coconut mixture. Bake at 350° till light golden brown, about 30 minutes. Remove from pans; cool right side up. Wrap in foil; freeze.
Before serving: Heat frozen cakes in foil wrap at 350° till warm through, 30 to 35 minutes. Open foil wrap during last 10 minutes of heating. Combine confectioners' sugar and orange juice; drizzle over cakes just before serving. Makes 2 cakes.

CHERRY COFFEE CAKE
35 minutes cooking time

1¼ cups sifted all-purpose flour
½ cup granulated sugar
1½ teaspoons baking powder
¼ teaspoon salt
¼ cup butter or margarine
1 beaten egg
3 tablespoons milk
1 teaspoon vanilla
1 21-ounce can cherry pie filling
• • •
½ cup sifted all-purpose flour
¼ cup brown sugar
½ teaspoon ground cinnamon
¼ cup butter or margarine

Advance preparation: In bowl sift together 1¼ cups all-purpose flour, granulated sugar, baking powder, and salt; cut in ¼ cup butter or margarine till mixture resembles coarse crumbs. Combine beaten egg, milk, and vanilla. Add to dry ingredients in bowl; mix well. Spread mixture evenly in greased 11x7x1½-inch pan; spoon cherry pie filling over batter mixture.

Combine ½ cup all-purpose flour, brown sugar, and cinnamon; cut in ¼ cup butter or margarine till mixture resembles coarse crumbs. Sprinkle over pie filling. Bake at 350° for 45 to 50 minutes. Cool for 10 minutes; remove from pan. Cool thoroughly. Wrap in foil; freeze.
Before serving: Heat frozen coffee cake in foil wrap at 350° till warmed through, about 30 to 35 minutes. Open foil wrap during the last 10 minutes of heating.

Coffee with a flair

Glamorize the weekly neighborhood coffee → with Cherry Coffee Cake and coffee topped with whipped cream and orange peel.

QUICK BREAD MIX

Keep mix on hand as a shortcut for preparing the recipes found on this page—

  10 cups sifted all-purpose flour
  ⅓ cup baking powder
  ¼ cup sugar
  1 tablespoon salt
  2 cups shortening that does not
      require refrigeration

Advance preparation: In large mixing bowl stir together flour, baking powder, sugar, and salt; sift together twice. Cut shortening into dry ingredients till mixture resembles coarse cornmeal. Store in covered container up to 6 weeks at room temperature. For longer storage, place in freezer.

  To measure, spoon mix into measuring cup; level with spatula. Makes 12 cups.

BASIC PANCAKES

 5 minutes to assemble
 10 minutes cooking time

  1 beaten egg
  1⅓ cups milk
  2 cups Quick Bread Mix

Before serving: Combine egg and milk; add Quick Bread Mix and beat smooth with rotary beater. Bake on hot, lightly greased griddle. Makes ten 4-inch pancakes.

BASIC DROP BISCUITS

 5 minutes to assemble
 10 minutes cooking time

  2 cups Quick Bread Mix
  ⅔ cup milk

Before serving: In mixing bowl make a well in Quick Bread Mix; add milk all at once. Stir quickly with fork just till dough follows fork around bowl. Drop dough from teaspoon onto greased baking sheet. Bake biscuits at 450° for 10 to 12 minutes. Makes 10 to 12 medium biscuits.

BASIC BISCUITS

 10 minutes to assemble
 10 minutes cooking time

  2 cups Quick Bread Mix
  ½ cup milk

Before serving: In mixing bowl make a well in Quick Bread Mix; add milk all at once. Stir quickly with fork just till dough follows fork around bowl. On lightly floured surface, knead dough 10 to 12 strokes. Roll or pat to ½-inch thickness. Dip biscuit cutter in flour; cut dough straight down. Bake on *ungreased* baking sheet at 450° for 10 to 12 minutes. Makes 10 biscuits.

BASIC MUFFINS

 5 minutes to assemble
 25 minutes cooking time

  3 cups Quick Bread Mix
  3 tablespoons sugar
  1 beaten egg
  1 cup milk

Before serving: In bowl combine Quick Bread Mix and sugar. Combine egg and milk; add all at once to dry ingredients. Stir just till dry ingredients are moistened. Fill greased muffin pans ⅔ full. Bake at 400° for 20 to 25 minutes. Makes 12 to 15.

BASIC WAFFLES

 10 minutes to assemble
 15 minutes cooking time

  2 beaten egg yolks
  1⅓ cups milk
  2 tablespoons salad oil or melted
      shortening
  2 cups Quick Bread Mix
  2 stiffly beaten egg whites

Before serving: Combine first 3 ingredients. Stir in Quick Bread Mix; beat smooth with rotary beater. Fold in egg whites, leaving a few fluffs. Bake in preheated waffle baker. Makes three 10-inch waffles.

RAISIN-SPICE MUFFINS

5 minutes to assemble
30 minutes cooking time

⅔ cup shortening
½ cup sugar
2 eggs
½ cup buttermilk or sour milk
½ cup light molasses
2 cups sifted all-purpose flour
1 teaspoon baking soda
½ teaspoon salt
½ teaspoon ground cinnamon
¼ teaspoon ground cloves
⅛ teaspoon ground nutmeg
1 cup raisins

Advance preparation: Cream shortening with sugar. Beat in eggs, milk, and molasses. Sift together dry ingredients; stir into batter. Fold in raisins. Store in casserole with tight-fitting lid. Batter may be refrigerated, covered, up to 10 days.
Before serving: *Without stirring batter,* fill greased muffin pans ⅔ full. Bake at 350° for 25 to 30 minutes. Makes 18 to 20.

DATE-NUT BREAD

No final preparation

1½ cups sifted all-purpose flour
1 teaspoon baking soda
½ teaspoon baking powder
½ teaspoon salt
¾ cup quick-cooking rolled oats
½ cup chopped walnuts
½ cup snipped dates
1 beaten egg
1 cup dairy sour cream
½ cup sugar
¼ cup light molasses

Advance preparation: Sift together first 4 ingredients in a mixing bowl. Stir in oats, nuts, and dates. Combine remaining ingredients; beat well. Add to dry ingredients; stir just till moistened. Place in 8½x4½x2½-inch loaf dish. Bake at 350° for 40 to 45 minutes. Remove from dish; cool. Wrap in foil; refrigerate. Makes 1 loaf.

Self-layering Apricot Nibble Bread combines a rich cream cheese filling with a convenient apricot-nut quick bread mix.

APRICOT NIBBLE BREAD

No final preparation

2 3-ounce packages cream cheese,
    softened
⅓ cup sugar
1 tablespoon all-purpose flour
1 egg
1 teaspoon grated orange peel
1 beaten egg
½ cup orange juice
½ cup water
1 17-ounce package apricot-nut
    quick bread mix

Advance preparation: Combine cream cheese, sugar, and flour; beat in the first egg and grated orange peel. Set mixture aside.

Combine the beaten egg, orange juice, and water. Add apricot-nut quick bread mix, stirring till moistened. Turn ⅔ of the apricot batter into a greased and floured 9x5x3-inch loaf pan. Pour cream cheese mixture over top of batter in pan; spoon on remaining apricot batter.

Bake at 350° for 1 hour. Cool for 10 minutes; remove from pan. Cool on rack. Wrap in foil; refrigerate. Makes 1 loaf.

CELERY-BREAD ROLLS
20 minutes cooking time

  1 small loaf unsliced white bread
  ½ cup butter or margarine, softened
  1 teaspoon celery seed
  ¼ teaspoon salt
  ¼ teaspoon paprika
    Dash cayenne

Advance preparation: Trim crusts from top, sides, and ends of loaf. Cut down through center of loaf, lengthwise, *almost to bottom crust.* Cut at 1-inch intervals, crosswise, *almost to bottom crust.* Combine butter and remaining ingredients. Spread over entire cut surfaces. Place on baking sheet; cover with waxed paper and chill.
Before serving: Uncover loaf and heat at 400° till golden, 15 to 18 minutes.

CHEESE LOAF
25 minutes cooking time

  1 unsliced loaf Italian bread
  6 tablespoons butter, softened
  1 tablespoon prepared horseradish
    Few drops bottled hot pepper sauce
  1 8-ounce package sharp process American cheese slices

Advance preparation: Cut bread diagonally into 1-inch slices. Cream butter with next 2 ingredients. Spread lightly on *all* cut surfaces of bread. Cut cheese slices in half diagonally; insert 1 triangle in each bread cut. Wrap in foil; chill or freeze.
Before serving: (Thaw frozen loaf at room temperature 2 to 3 hours.) Heat in foil at 400° till cheese melts, 25 minutes.

Prepared in advance, crisp and buttery Celery-Bread Rolls are a jiffy bread fix-up. Generously spread with a celery seed butter, the rolls toast in the oven just before serving.

BROWN-AND-SERVE ROLLS
10 minutes cooking time

> **1 package active dry yeast**
> **3½ cups sifted all-purpose flour**
> **1¼ cups milk**
> **¼ cup sugar**
> **¼ cup shortening**
> **1 teaspoon salt**
> **1 egg**

Advance preparation: In large mixer bowl combine yeast and *2 cups* of the flour. In saucepan heat milk, sugar, shortening, and salt till warm, stirring occasionally to melt shortening. Add to dry mixture in mixing bowl; add egg. Beat at low speed with electric mixer for ½ minute, scraping sides of bowl constantly. Beat 3 minutes at high speed. By hand, stir in enough of the remaining flour to make a soft dough.

Place dough in greased bowl, turning once to grease surface. Cover and let rise till double, 1½ to 2 hours. Turn onto lightly floured surface; shape into rolls, as desired. Place on greased baking sheet or in greased muffin pans. Cover; let rise till double, 30 to 45 minutes. Bake at 325° for 15 minutes; *do not brown.* Remove from pan; cool. Wrap and freeze.

Before serving: Thaw wrapped rolls at room temperature 10 to 15 minutes. Unwrap; bake at 450° till golden brown, 5 to 10 minutes. Makes 24 Cloverleaves, Butter Fans, or Bowknots; or 36 Parker House rolls.

REFRIGERATOR ROLLS
15 minutes cooking time

Advance preparation: Prepare dough for Brown-and-Serve Rolls (above). *Do not let rise.* Place dough in greased bowl, turning once to grease surface. Cover; chill at least 2 hours, or up to 5 days.

Before serving: About 2 hours before baking, shape into rolls on floured surface, as desired. Place rolls on greased baking sheet or in greased muffin pans. Cover; let rise till double, about 1¼ hours. Bake rolls at 400° for 12 to 15 minutes.

SEASONED HERB LOAF
20 minutes cooking time

> **1 unsliced loaf French bread**
> **(about 1 pound)**
> • • •
> **½ cup butter or margarine, softened**
> **1 tablespoon grated onion**
> **½ teaspoon poultry seasoning**

Advance preparation: Cut bread diagonally into 1-inch slices. Blend butter, onion, and poultry seasoning; spread on *one* cut surface of each bread slice. Reassemble loaf; wrap in foil. Refrigerate or freeze.

Before serving: (Thaw frozen loaf at room temperature 2 to 3 hours.) Heat at 400° for 20 minutes. Or heat on edge of grill till hot, about 20 minutes; turn often.

 TIMELY TIPS

● Prepare bread crumbs in quantity by blending leftover slices of bread in blender container. Store bread crumbs in the refrigerator or freezer to use as a jiffy casserole topper or to use in meat loaf mixtures.

● When freezer space is available, take advantage of cool weather to bake and freeze an assortment of yeast and quick breads.

● Divide and package sweet rolls, muffins, and other individual breads in meal-sized portions before refrigerating or freezing to avoid unnecessary thawing and warming.

● Wrap bread in foil before freezing or refrigerating to eliminate rewrapping of bread before popping into the oven to warm.

● Freeze coffee cakes, sweet rolls, and special holiday breads unfrosted. After thawing and heating, drizzle warm bread with confectioners' glaze, if desired.

● Fruit and nut breads generally improve in flavor when baked a few days before serving. To prepare nut bread sandwiches in advance, thinly slice bread and spread with softened cream cheese, butter, or margarine; freeze sandwiches till needed.

DESSERTS THAT WAIT

RASPBERRY CREPES

10 minutes cooking time

⅓ cup sifted all-purpose flour
1 tablespoon sugar
¾ cup milk
1 egg
1 egg yolk
1 tablespoon butter or margarine, melted
¼ teaspoon almond extract
1 4-ounce container whipped cream cheese, softened
⅓ cup toasted, slivered almonds
1 10-ounce package frozen red raspberries, thawed
  Cranberry juice cocktail
⅓ cup sugar
4 teaspoons cornstarch
2 tablespoons butter or margarine
2 tablespoons orange-flavored liqueur (optional)
2 teaspoons lemon juice

Advance preparation: Combine first 7 ingredients and dash salt; beat smooth. Lightly grease a 6-inch skillet; heat. Remove from heat. Add 2 tablespoons batter; tilt pan to spread evenly over bottom. Return to heat; brown on one side only. To remove, invert over paper toweling. Repeat with remaining batter, greasing pan as needed.

Spread unbrowned side of crepes with cream cheese. Sprinkle with 4 *tablespoons* of the almonds. Roll up crepes. Cover; chill.

Drain berries; reserve syrup. Add cranberry juice to syrup to equal 1½ cups. Combine ⅓ cup sugar, cornstarch, and dash salt; blend in juice. Cook and stir till bubbly. Add 2 tablespoons butter, liqueur, lemon juice, and berries. Cover; chill.

Before serving: Heat sauce in saucepan. Put crepes in blazer pan of chafing dish or in skillet. Pour hot sauce over crepes; cover and heat through over direct heat. Garnish with remaining almonds. Serves 5.

PLUM-CHERRY COMPOTE

5 minutes final preparation

1 17-ounce can whole, unpitted purple plums
1 16-ounce can pitted dark sweet cherries
• • •
2 tablespoons sugar
1 tablespoon cornstarch
½ cup orange juice
5 inches stick cinnamon
1 thin lemon slice
• • •
⅓ cup dry sherry
½ cup dairy sour cream

Advance preparation: Drain purple plums and dark sweet cherries, reserving syrups. In 1½-quart saucepan blend sugar and cornstarch together. Gradually stir in orange juice and reserved fruit syrups. Add stick cinnamon and lemon slice. Cook over medium heat, stirring constantly, till mixture is thickened and bubbly. Cook and stir 2 to 3 minutes longer. Remove sauce from heat; discard stick cinnamon and lemon slice. Cool slightly.

Stir dry sherry into the sauce mixture in saucepan. Place purple plums and dark sweet cherries in a medium bowl; pour the sauce mixture over the fruit. Cover and refrigerate till chilled thoroughly, stirring fruit mixture occasionally.

Before serving: Spoon the fruit and sauce mixture into individual dessert dishes. Top each serving with a dollop of sour cream. Makes 8 servings.

For special occasions

Add a glamorous touch to a dinner by serving Raspberry Crepes. Heat the crepes and sauce in a chafing dish at the dinner table. →

CREAMY RIBBON LOAF
No final preparation

1 3¼-ounce package regular coconut
    cream pudding mix
1 envelope unflavored gelatin
    (1 tablespoon)
2 cups milk
1 pint vanilla ice cream, softened
16 thin chocolate wafers

Advance preparation: Combine pudding and gelatin. Add milk; cook and stir till mixture thickens and boils. Cool 5 minutes, stirring once or twice. Add ice cream. Stir till melted. Chill till slightly thickened. Spoon ⅓ of the pudding into 8½x4½x2⅝-inch loaf pan. Top with 6 wafers. Repeat layers of pudding, wafers, and then pudding. Crush remaining wafers; sprinkle over top. Cover; chill till set.
Before serving: Unmold onto serving plate. Garnish with whipped cream and chocolate curls, if desired. Makes 8 servings.

CHOCOLATE CHEESECAKE
No final preparation

1 10¾- or 11-ounce package
    cheesecake mix
¼ cup butter or margarine, melted
4 tablespoons sugar
1½ cups cold milk
1 1-ounce envelope no-melt
    unsweetened chocolate
½ cup dairy sour cream

Advance preparation: Combine crumbs from cheesecake mix, butter, and *3 tablespoons* of the sugar. Press crumb mixture onto bottom and 1 inch up sides of 7½-inch springform pan. Chill. Combine milk, packaged filling mix, and remaining sugar. Beat at low speed of electric mixer till blended; beat at medium speed for 3 minutes. Add chocolate; beat at low speed 1 minute more. Pour into crust; spread sour cream over top. Cover; chill at least 1 hour.
Before serving: Garnish with chocolate curls, if desired. Makes 6 to 8 servings.

RHUBARB CHEESECAKE
No final preparation

As pictured opposite contents page —

Crumb Crust
3 well-beaten eggs
2 8-ounce packages cream cheese,
    softened
1⅓ cups sugar
2 teaspoons vanilla
½ teaspoon ground nutmeg
¼ teaspoon salt
3 cups dairy sour cream
• • •
1 cup fresh rhubarb, cut in 1-inch
    pieces (¼ pound)
1 tablespoon cornstarch
Dash salt
7 or 8 drops red food coloring
2 cups fresh strawberries, halved

Advance preparation: Prepare Crumb Crust. In bowl combine eggs, cream cheese, *1 cup* of the sugar, vanilla, nutmeg, and the ¼ teaspoon salt; beat till smooth. Blend in sour cream. Pour into Crumb Crust. Bake at 375° just till set, 40 to 45 minutes. (Filling will be soft.) Cool.

In saucepan combine rhubarb, remaining ⅓ cup sugar, and ½ cup water. Bring to boiling; reduce heat. Simmer, uncovered, till almost tender, about 1 minute, being careful not to break up rhubarb. Remove from heat. Drain, reserving syrup. Add water to syrup to equal ¾ cup. Mix cornstarch, dash salt, and 2 tablespoons cold water; add to syrup mixture. Cook and stir till thick and bubbly; cook 1 minute more. Remove glaze from heat; stir in food coloring. Cool to room temperature.

Arrange strawberries and rhubarb on cooled cheesecake. Spoon glaze over the top. Cover and chill. Makes 12 servings.
Crumb Crust: Combine 1½ cups zwieback crumbs; ⅓ cup sugar; ¾ teaspoon ground cinnamon; and 6 tablespoons butter or margarine, melted. Mix till crumbly. Press crumbs on bottom and about 1½ inches up the sides of a buttered 9-inch springform pan. Chill crumb crust thoroughly.

STRAWBERRY PINK CLOUD
No final preparation

A double strawberry treat—

   4 cups sliced fresh strawberries
   ½ cup sugar
   ¼ cup sugar
   1 envelope unflavored gelatin
      (1 tablespoon)
   ⅛ teaspoon salt
   4 beaten egg yolks
   1 tablespoon lemon juice
   7 or 8 drops red food coloring
   4 egg whites
   ¼ cup sugar
   ½ cup whipping cream
   ⅓ cup sugar
   1 tablespoon cornstarch
   ⅛ teaspoon salt
   ⅛ teaspoon ground allspice
   3 tablespoons orange-flavored
      liqueur
   ½ teaspoon lemon peel
   1 teaspoon lemon juice

Advance preparation: Sprinkle *2 cups* of the strawberries with ½ cup sugar; let stand till syrup forms, about 1 hour. In saucepan blend the ¼ cup sugar, gelatin, and ⅛ teaspoon salt. Stir in ½ cup water, syrup from berries, and egg yolks. Cook and stir over low heat till gelatin dissolves and mixture thickens slightly. Remove from heat; stir in the sweetened berries, 1 tablespoon lemon juice, and food coloring. Chill till mixture mounds.

Beat egg whites to soft peaks; gradually add ¼ cup sugar, beating to stiff peaks. Whip cream; fold into strawberry mixture along with egg whites. Turn into 6½-cup mold. Cover; chill till firm, at least 6 hours.

In saucepan combine ⅓ cup sugar, cornstarch, ⅛ teaspoon salt, and allspice; add 1 cup water. Cook and stir till thickened and bubbly; cook and stir 5 minutes more. Add remaining 2 cups strawberries, orange liqueur, lemon peel, and 1 teaspoon lemon juice; stir gently. Cover; chill.

Before serving: Unmold dessert onto platter; pass sauce. Makes 10 servings.

Wrap a wide strip of foil around the top of the soufflé dish so Orange Soufflé will stand high above the edge when firm.

ORANGE SOUFFLÉ
No final preparation

   ½ cup sugar
   1 envelope unflavored gelatin
      (1 tablespoon)
   3 eggs, separated
   ⅓ cup orange-flavor breakfast
      drink powder
   1 2-ounce envelope dessert
      topping mix

Advance preparation: Combine ¼ cup of the sugar, gelatin, and ⅛ teaspoon salt; add 1½ cups cold water. Bring to boiling. Beat egg yolks; stir small amount of hot mixture into yolks. Return egg mixture to saucepan. Cook and stir over low heat till mixture coats metal spoon, 2 to 3 minutes. Remove from heat; stir in drink powder. Chill till partially set, stir occasionally.

Prepare topping mix according to package directions; fold into gelatin. Beat egg whites to soft peaks. Gradually add remaining sugar, beating to stiff peaks. Fold into gelatin mixture. Turn into 5-cup soufflé dish with a foil collar. Cover; chill till firm, at least 6 hours.

Before serving: Remove collar. Garnish with chocolate curls, if desired. Serves 8.

COFFEE ÉCLAIRS
10 minutes to assemble
10 minutes cooking time

- ½ cup butter or margarine
- 1 cup boiling water
- 1 cup sifted all-purpose flour
- 4 eggs
- 1 quart vanilla or coffee ice cream

• • •

- 1 cup light corn syrup
- 1½ cups water
- 1 tablespoon instant coffee powder
- 3 tablespoons cornstarch
- 2 tablespoons butter or margarine
- 1 teaspoon vanilla
- ½ cup chopped pecans

Advance preparation: In saucepan combine the ½ cup butter or margarine and the 1 cup boiling water; bring to boiling. Add flour all at once, stirring rapidly. Reduce heat. Cook and stir till mixture leaves sides of pan and gathers around spoon in smooth, compact mass. Remove saucepan from heat. Add eggs, one at a time, beat vigorously after each addition. Continue beating till éclair mixture looks satiny and breaks off when spoon is raised.

Using about ¼ cup dough for each éclair, drop dough onto *ungreased* baking sheet about 2 inches apart, leaving about 6 inches space between rows. (Make 10 to 12 éclairs.) With small spatula, shape each mound into a 4x1-inch rectangle, rounding sides and piling dough on top. Bake at 400° till deep golden brown and puffy, about 40 minutes. Cool éclairs on rack.

Cut each éclair in half lengthwise and remove webbing from inside. Fill bottom halves of éclairs with vanilla ice cream; replace tops. Cover and freeze.

Before serving: Pour corn syrup into saucepan. Combine the 1½ cups water and coffee powder; blend in cornstarch. Stir into corn syrup. Cook and stir till sauce thickens and boils; cook 2 minutes more. Remove from heat; add the 2 tablespoons butter and vanilla. Stir till butter melts; add pecans. Serve sauce warm over frozen éclairs. Makes 10 to 12 servings.

Delight your family or guests with a special frozen dessert—Coffee Éclairs filled with either coffee ice cream or vanilla ice cream.

COFFEE-TOFFEE SQUARES
No final preparation

    1 cup chocolate wafer crumbs
    2 tablespoons butter or margarine,
        melted
    ½ cup butter or margarine
    ½ cup sugar
    4 egg yolks
    1 1-ounce square unsweetened
        chocolate, melted and cooled
    2 teaspoons instant coffee powder
    ½ teaspoon vanilla
            • • •
    4 egg whites
    ¼ cup sugar
    3 ¾-ounce chocolate-covered
        toffee bars

Advance preparation: Combine crumbs and the melted butter; press into bottom of 8x8x2-inch baking pan. Cream together the ½ cup butter and the ½ cup sugar till light and fluffy. Thoroughly beat in egg yolks, chocolate, coffee powder, and vanilla.

Beat egg whites till soft peaks form; gradually add the ¼ cup sugar, beating till stiff peaks form. Fold egg white mixture into chocolate mixture. Spread over crumb crust. Coarsely crush toffee bars; sprinkle over chocolate mixture. Cover; freeze till firm. Makes 6 to 8 servings.

CRAN-MALLOW DESSERT
No final preparation

    1 16-ounce can whole cranberry
        sauce
    1 7-ounce jar marshmallow creme
    ½ cup whipping cream
    1 tablespoon lemon juice

Advance preparation: In bowl beat cranberry sauce into marshmallow creme. Turn mixture into 3-cup refrigerator tray; freeze till firm. Whip cream. Place frozen mixture in chilled bowl, breaking into chunks. Add lemon juice; beat till fluffy. Fold in whipping cream. Return to refrigerator tray. Cover; freeze till firm. Makes 1 quart.

QUICK TORTONI CUPS
No final preparation

    1 quart vanilla ice cream, softened
    ½ cup slivered almonds, toasted
    1 ⅞-ounce milk chocolate candy bar,
        chopped
    2 tablespoons chopped maraschino
        cherries
    ½ teaspoon brandy flavoring
    ¼ teaspoon grated orange peel
    ¼ teaspoon grated lemon peel

Advance preparation: Combine all ingredients. Pile into 10 paper bake cups in muffin pans. Cover; freeze firm. Serves 10.

STRAWBERRY PARFAITS
10 minutes to assemble

    1 pint fresh strawberries
    ½ envelope unflavored gelatin
        (1½ teaspoons)
    2 tablespoons cold water
    2 cups buttermilk
    ¾ cup sugar
    ½ teaspoon vanilla
    1 or 2 drops red food coloring
    2 egg whites
    ⅓ cup sugar
    1 pint fresh strawberries

Advance preparation: Push 1 pint strawberries through food mill or sieve to make purée. Soften gelatin in cold water; heat over hot water till dissolved. Combine buttermilk, ¾ cup sugar, strawberry purée, vanilla, food coloring, and gelatin; mix well. Turn into one 6-cup or two 3-cup refrigerator trays. Cover; freeze firm.

Beat egg whites to soft peaks. Gradually add ⅓ cup sugar, beating to stiff peaks. Break frozen mixture into chunks; turn into chilled bowl. Beat smooth. Fold whites into frozen mixture. Return to cold refrigerator tray. Cover; freeze firm.
Before serving: Slice remaining 1 pint strawberries; sweeten to taste. Spoon sherbet and berries alternately into parfait glasses. Serve immediately. Serves 7 or 8.

ICE CREAM ROLL
No final preparation

   2 cups soft coconut macaroon crumbs
        (9 macaroons)
 ¼ cup dry sherry
   1 quart vanilla ice cream, softened
   1 cup dairy sour cream
   4 egg whites
 ½ cup granulated sugar
   4 egg yolks
 ¼ cup granulated sugar
 ½ teaspoon vanilla
 ⅔ cup sifted cake flour
   1 teaspoon baking powder
 ¼ cup cocoa powder
 ¼ teaspoon salt
       Sifted confectioners' sugar

Advance preparation: Combine macaroon crumbs and sherry. Stir into softened ice cream. Add sour cream; mix well. Freeze.

Beat egg whites to soft peaks; add ½ cup granulated sugar; beat to stiff peaks. Beat yolks till thick and lemon colored; beat in ¼ cup granulated sugar. Add vanilla. Fold into whites. Sift together flour and next 3 ingredients; fold into egg mixture. Spread in greased and lightly floured 15½x10½x1-inch jelly roll pan. Bake at 375° for 10 to 12 minutes. Immediately turn out on towel sprinkled with confectioners' sugar. Starting at narrow end, roll cake and towel together. Cool on rack.

Stir sherried ice cream to soften. Unroll jelly roll and spread with ice cream. Roll up; wrap in foil. Freeze. Serves 10 to 12.

Create a modern version of the classic Charlotte Russe using convenience products. Packaged ladyfingers and pudding mix shorten the preparation once necessary to make this dessert.

CHARLOTTE RUSSE
5 minutes final preparation

1 4½- or 5-ounce package regular
    vanilla pudding mix
1 teaspoon unflavored gelatin
2 cups milk
1 4-ounce bar sweet baking chocolate,
    broken into squares
1½ cups whipping cream
2 3-ounce packages ladyfingers (16),
    split

Advance preparation: Combine pudding mix and gelatin; stir in milk. Cook and stir over medium heat till boiling. Remove from heat. Add chocolate; stir till melted. Cool thoroughly; then beat smooth.

Whip *1 cup* of the cream; fold into pudding. Line an 8½x4½x2½-inch loaf dish with waxed paper, extending paper beyond rim. Line bottom and sides of dish with ladyfinger halves. Pour in *half* of the pudding. Add a layer of ladyfinger halves and then remaining pudding. Top with remaining ladyfinger halves. Chill till mixture is firm, at least 4 hours.

Before serving: Grasping waxed paper, lift dessert from dish and carefully transfer to plate; remove waxed paper. Whip remaining cream; spoon over dessert. Serves 6.

CHERRY-ANGEL TREAT
No final preparation

1 cup sifted confectioners' sugar
1 3-ounce package cream cheese,
    softened
1 2-ounce envelope dessert
    topping mix
5 cups angel cake cubes
1 21-ounce can cherry pie filling

Advance preparation: Beat confectioners' sugar with cream cheese till fluffy. Prepare topping mix according to package directions; fold into cheese mixture with cake cubes. Turn into 11x7x1½-inch baking pan. Spread pie filling over top. Cover; chill at least 2 to 3 hours. Makes 9 servings.

PINK LEMONADE CAKE
No final preparation

1 package 2-layer-size yellow
    cake mix
1 quart vanilla ice cream
6 drops red food coloring
1 6-ounce can frozen pink lemonade
    concentrate, thawed
1 cup whipping cream
2 tablespoons sugar

Advance preparation: Prepare cake mix according to package directions; bake in two 9x1½-inch round cake pans. Cool. Stir ice cream to soften; quickly stir in food coloring and ½ cup of the lemonade concentrate. Spread ice cream mixture evenly in foil-lined 9x1½-inch round cake pan. Freeze till firm, 2 to 3 hours.

Place one cake layer on plate; top with ice cream layer, then second cake layer. Whip cream with remaining lemonade and sugar till stiff. Frost sides and top of cake. Return to freezer at least 1 hour.

CHOCOLATE DELIGHT
No final preparation

1 envelope unflavored gelatin
    (1 tablespoon)
½ cup cold water
1 package fluffy chocolate frosting
    mix
1 cup whipping cream
4 cups angel cake cubes
¼ cup chopped peanuts

Advance preparation: Soften gelatin in cold water; dissolve over hot water. Remove from heat. Prepare frosting mix according to package directions; blend in gelatin. Chill, stirring occasionally, till mixture mounds. Whip cream; fold into chocolate mixture with cake cubes. Sprinkle peanuts in bottom of oiled 5½- or 6½-cup mold. Spoon in chocolate mixture. Chill till firm, at least 5 hours.

Before serving: Unmold onto plate; top with additional nuts, if desired. Serves 8.

Named for Hawaii's last king, King Kamehameha Pie blends the flavor of the islands' pineapple juice with the flavor of the mainland's apples for a superb dessert to serve anywhere.

STRAWBERRY-CHEESE PIE
No final preparation

1 cup miniature marshmallows
½ cup milk
1 3-ounce package strawberry-flavored gelatin
1 3-ounce package cream cheese, softened
1 10-ounce package frozen strawberries, thawed
½ cup whipping cream
1 baked 9-inch pastry shell, cooled

Advance preparation: In saucepan heat marshmallows and milk over low heat, stirring frequently, till marshmallows are melted. Cool. Combine gelatin and ½ cup water; heat and stir till gelatin is dissolved. Combine marshmallow mixture and gelatin; gradually beat into cream cheese. Drain berries; reserve syrup. Add water to syrup to equal 1 cup; stir into gelatin mixture. Chill till partially set. Whip gelatin mixture; fold in berries. Whip cream; fold into whipped gelatin. Pour into pastry shell. Cover; chill till pie is set.

FROSTY FUDGE PIE
No final preparation

Advance preparation: Beat 1 egg white to soft peaks. Gradually add ¼ cup brown sugar, beating to stiff peaks. Fold in 2 cups wheat flake cereal, crushed (1 cup), and ½ cup finely chopped walnuts. Press in *ungreased* 9-inch pie plate. Bake at 300° for 10 minutes. Cool.

In saucepan combine 1 cup milk; two 1-ounce squares unsweetened chocolate, cut up; and dash salt. Stir over low heat till chocolate melts. Add ½ pound marshmallows (32 regular or 4 cups miniature); stir till melted. Stir small amount of hot mixture into 1 beaten egg yolk; return to hot mixture. Cook and stir over low heat 1 minute more. Add 1 teaspoon vanilla. Chill till partially set; stir occasionally.

Whip 1 cup whipping cream; fold into chocolate mixture. Chill till mixture mounds. Turn into crust. Cover; freeze.
Before serving: Let pie stand at room temperature 15 minutes before cutting.

LEMON-BLUEBERRY PIE
No final preparation

Advance preparation: Mix 1 cup sifted all-purpose flour, ½ cup butter or margarine, 2 tablespoons sugar, and 1 teaspoon salt till crumbly. Place ⅓ cup of the crumb mixture in a baking dish; press remaining crumb mixture into greased and floured 9-inch pie plate. Bake both at 375° for 12 to 15 minutes; cool.

Combine 2 egg whites, ⅔ cup sugar, 2 teaspoons grated lemon peel, ¼ cup lemon juice, and 5 drops yellow food coloring; beat to stiff peaks with electric mixer. Whip 1 cup whipping cream; fold into mixture. Turn into crumb crust; top with remaining crumbs. Cover; chill.

Combine ⅔ cup sugar, 1 tablespoon cornstarch, and dash salt. Add ⅔ cup water. Cook and stir till thick and bubbly; cook 2 minutes more. Add 2 cups fresh blueberries; return to boiling. Cover; chill.
Before serving: Serve sauce over pie.

KING KAMEHAMEHA PIE
No final preparation

- 1 12-ounce can pineapple juice
- ¾ cup sugar
- 7 medium tart apples, peeled, cored, and cut in wedges (7 cups)
- 3 tablespoons cornstarch
- 1 tablespoon butter or margarine
- ½ teaspoon vanilla
- ¼ teaspoon salt
- 1 baked 9-inch pastry shell, cooled

Advance preparation: In large saucepan combine 1¼ *cups* of the pineapple juice and sugar. Bring to boiling; add apples. Simmer, covered, till tender but not soft, 3 to 4 minutes. Lift apples from syrup; set aside to drain. Combine cornstarch and remaining pineapple juice; add to syrup in saucepan. Cook and stir till thick and bubbly; cook 1 minute more. Remove from heat; add butter, vanilla, and salt. Cool 10 minutes without stirring. Pour *half* of the syrup into pastry shell; spread to cover bottom. Arrange apples atop. Spoon remaining syrup over apples. Cover; chill.
Before serving: Garnish pie with whipped cream and macadamia nuts, if desired.

 TIMELY TIPS

- To keep fresh fruits (peaches, pears, and bananas) bright, dip in ascorbic acid color keeper or lemon juice mixed with water.
- To avoid whipping cream at the last minute, whip cream several days ahead and mound on waxed paper-lined baking sheet. Freeze till firm; transfer to freezer container. To serve, place a mound on each dessert; let stand at room temperature 20 minutes before serving.
- Keep toasted nuts and coconut, chopped nuts, and/or tinted coconut on hand for use in desserts or as a quick dessert garnish.
- Hasten the preparation of crepe desserts by freezing crepes in advance. Let crepes thaw at room temperature before filling.

make-ahead Meals For Entertaining

Would you like to entertain more often but just don't have the time? Try spacing out the preparation so that most of the food is ready in advance of party time. Also, organize those steps that must be done at the last minute to eliminate confusion. In this section, you'll find party menus and guides for getting each one ready effortlessly. Try some of these and see how much easier it is to give a make-ahead party. Chances are you'll be entertaining more and having more fun, too.

Golden Fruit Punch, Meatball Nuggets, Appetizer Cheesecake, Artichokes with Dip, and Chicken-Ham Pinwheels are featured in the Appetizer Buffet.

APPETIZER BUFFET

COUNTDOWN
FROM KITCHEN TO TABLE

Several days before party, prepare Meatball Nuggets and freeze. Day before party, follow advance preparation instructions for remaining appetizers and punch. Select table appointments and serving dishes.

Time before serving:

45 minutes Set table.

40 minutes Bake Meatball Nuggets.

35 minutes Slice Chicken-Ham Pinwheels.

30 minutes Arrange all appetizers in serving dishes.

5 minutes Complete preparation of Golden Fruit Punch.

Invite guests to buffet table.

VEGETABLE DIPPERS
No final preparation

Advance preparation: Select a variety of crisp and colorful vegetables to serve as dippers—sliced cauliflowerets, cherry tomatoes with stems, whole fresh mushrooms, celery sticks, cucumber wedges, carrot sticks, or green onions with tops. Wash and prepare vegetables; refrigerate in plastic bags until serving time.

CHICKEN-HAM PINWHEELS
5 minutes final preparation

2 chicken breasts, skinned and
   boned
⅛ teaspoon salt
⅛ teaspoon dried basil leaves,
   crushed
Dash pepper
Dash garlic salt
3 slices boiled ham
2 teaspoons lemon juice
Paprika

Advance preparation: Pound chicken breasts, skinned side down, to ¼-inch thickness. Mix salt, basil, pepper, and garlic salt; sprinkle on chicken. Cover each chicken breast with 1½ slices ham; roll up lengthwise. Place, seam side down, in 10x6x1¾-inch baking dish. Drizzle with lemon juice; sprinkle with paprika. Bake at 350° for 35 to 40 minutes. Cover; chill thoroughly.
Before serving: Cut chicken rolls into ¼-inch slices. If desired, serve with party rye bread spread with softened butter and prepared mustard. Makes 24 slices.

CRAB DIP
No final preparation

1 8-ounce package cream cheese,
   softened
¼ cup mayonnaise or salad dressing
¼ cup cocktail sauce
2 teaspoons prepared mustard
1 7½-ounce can crab meat, drained,
   flaked, and cartilage removed
⅓ cup finely chopped celery
2 tablespoons snipped parsley

Advance preparation: Blend cream cheese with mayonnaise, cocktail sauce, and mustard. Stir in crab, celery, and parsley. Cover; chill thoroughly. Makes 2 cups.

MEATBALL NUGGETS
40 minutes cooking time

2 cups soft bread crumbs
(about 2½ slices)
⅓ cup milk
1 tablespoon soy sauce
½ teaspoon garlic salt
¼ teaspoon onion powder
½ pound ground beef
½ pound bulk pork sausage
1 5-ounce can water chestnuts,
drained and finely chopped

Advance preparation: Combine first 5 ingredients; add remaining ingredients and mix well. Form into 1-inch balls. Place on cookie sheet and freeze firm; wrap in foil or plastic bag and return to freezer.
Before serving: Place frozen meatballs on 15½x10½x1-inch baking pan. Bake at 350° for 35 to 40 minutes. Keep warm in chafing dish. Makes about 5 dozen.

APPETIZER CHEESECAKE
5 minutes final preparation

2 cups dairy sour cream
½ cup finely chopped green pepper
½ cup finely chopped celery
¼ cup finely chopped pimiento-
stuffed green olives
¼ cup finely chopped onion
2 teaspoons lemon juice
1 teaspoon Worcestershire sauce
Dash paprika
5 drops bottled hot pepper sauce
1⅓ cups rich round cracker crumbs

Advance preparation: Combine all ingredients except crumbs. Line 4-cup bowl with clear plastic wrap. Spread ½ cup of the sour cream mixture in bottom of bowl. Layer with ½ cup of the crumbs; then 1 cup sour cream mixture, ½ cup crumbs, and remaining sour cream mixture. Cover; chill for 24 hours. Store remaining cracker crumbs.
Before serving: Unmold onto serving plate; remove wrap. Top with remaining crumbs. Serve with assorted crackers, if desired.

ARTICHOKES WITH DIP
5 minutes final preparation

Whole fresh artichokes
Lemon juice
1 3-ounce package cream cheese,
softened
1 cup dairy sour cream
2 tablespoons finely snipped chives
2 tablespoons snipped parsley
1 tablespoon anchovy paste
2 teaspoons lemon juice
1 small clove garlic, minced
Dash freshly ground pepper

Advance preparation: Wash artichokes; cut stems to 1-inch length. Remove loose outer leaves. Cut off 1 inch from top; snip off thorny tips of leaves. Brush cut edges with lemon juice. Add artichokes to boiling, salted water. Cover; simmer till stems are tender and leaf pulls easily from base, 20 to 30 minutes. Drain; cover and chill.

Blend softened cream cheese with sour cream. Stir in chives and remaining ingredients; mix well. Cover and chill.
Before serving: Arrange artichokes on serving plate with dip. Makes 1¼ cups dip.

GOLDEN FRUIT PUNCH
5 minutes final preparation

2 6-ounce cans frozen orange juice
concentrate, thawed
1 6-ounce can frozen pineapple
juice concentrate, thawed
1 pint light rum (2 cups)*
2 cups water
1 28-ounce bottle ginger ale,
chilled (3½ cups)
1 quart lemon or pineapple sherbet

Advance preparation: Combine concentrates, rum, and water. Cover and chill.
Before serving: Pour juice mixture into punch bowl. Slowly pour ginger ale down side of bowl; stir with an up-and-down motion. Scoop sherbet into punch. Serves 24.
*Or substitute 2 cups water for rum, using a total of 4 cups water in punch.

FONDUE EVENING

COUNTDOWN
FROM KITCHEN TO TABLE

Day before serving, marinate fondue cubes and prepare sundae sauce. Cover and chill.
Two hours before dinner, wrap meat cubes; scoop sherbet into dishes, freeze.

Time before serving:

30 minutes Set out sundae sauce. Start coffee. Set table.

20 minutes Prepare tossed salad.

10 minutes Heat oil. Heat marinade.

5 minutes Pour beverage. Serve food.

Invite guests to table.

TROPICAL SUNDAES
No final preparation

1 7-ounce jar marshmallow creme
3 tablespoons light rum
¼ cup flaked coconut
   Raspberry, pineapple, and lime
   sherbet

Advance preparation: Heat and stir marshmallow creme till softened; blend in rum and coconut; cool. Cover and refrigerate.
Place a small scoop of *each* sherbet into each dessert dish; return to freezer.
Before serving: Allow sauce to come to room temperature; stir. Drizzle over sherbet in *each* dish. Makes 1⅓ cups sauce.

FONDUE WELLINGTON
10 minutes final preparation

1½ pounds beef tenderloin, trimmed
     and cut into 1-inch cubes
⅔ cup red wine vinegar
¼ cup catsup
2 tablespoons soy sauce
1 medium onion, sliced
1 small clove garlic, minced
½ teaspoon dry mustard
2 tubes refrigerated crescent rolls
   (16 rolls)
1 4¾-ounce can liverwurst spread
   Salad oil

Advance preparation: In skillet cook meat, uncovered, over medium-high heat till medium done, about 12 minutes; turn occasionally. Drain. Mix vinegar, next 5 ingredients, and ⅓ cup water; add meat. Cover and chill overnight; stir occasionally.
Two hours before serving, drain meat; reserve marinade. For *each tube* of rolls, separate dough into 4 rectangles; pinch together well along perforations. Spread liverwurst on dough to within ¼ inch of edges. Cut each rectangle into fourths. Place a meat cube on each quarter of dough; fold dough over meat; seal. Repeat for remaining dough. Let stand at room temperature.
Before serving: Pour oil into fondue cooker to no more than ½ capacity or to depth of 2 inches. Heat over range to 375°. Add 1 teaspoon salt; transfer to fondue burner. Using fondue fork, cook meat in hot oil 2 to 2½ minutes. Meanwhile, strain reserved marinade. Heat; use for dipping. Makes 32.

Fun with fondue

Assembled before guests arrive, Fondue →
Wellington gives a relaxed atmosphere to the party as guests help with the cooking.

DINNER PARTY

CHICKEN KIEV
25 minutes cooking time

> **4 large chicken breasts**
> **1 tablespoon chopped green onion**
> **1 tablespoon snipped parsley**
> **1 ¼-pound stick butter, well chilled**
> **¼ cup all-purpose flour**
> **1 beaten egg**
> **½ cup fine dry bread crumbs**
> **¼ cup butter**

COUNTDOWN
FROM KITCHEN TO TABLE

Day before dinner, follow advance preparation for soup, main dish, salad, and dessert. Select table appointments and serving dishes. Next morning, complete dessert.

Time before serving:

35 minutes Complete Chicken Kiev.

25 minutes Prepare beverage; set table.

15 minutes Cook corn. Bake rolls.

10 minutes Unmold salad; refrigerate.

5 minutes Put food in serving dishes; keep warm. Serve soup.

Invite guests to dinner table.

Advance preparation: Skin and bone chicken breasts; halve lengthwise. Place each half, bone side up, between two pieces clear plastic wrap. Pound out from center to ⅛-inch thickness; peel off wrap. Repeat with remaining breasts. Sprinkle chicken with salt, pepper, onion, and parsley.

Cut the well-chilled butter into 8 sticks, each about 2½ inches long. Place a stick on each piece chicken. Roll up jelly-roll fashion, tucking in ends; press to seal. Coat rolls with flour; dip in egg, then roll in bread crumbs. Cover; chill thoroughly.

Before serving: In skillet melt ¼ cup butter. Brown *cold* chicken rolls on all sides in hot butter, about 5 minutes. Transfer to 11¾x7½x1¾-inch baking dish. Bake at 400° for 15 to 20 minutes. Makes 8 servings.

CREAM OF CHIVE SOUP
No final preparation

Advance preparation: Melt 3 tablespoons butter; blend in 3 tablespoons all-purpose flour. Add one 13¾-ounce can chicken broth (1¾ cups); 3 tablespoons finely snipped chives; and 1 bay leaf. Cool and stir over medium heat till thick and bubbly. Cover; simmer 10 minutes. Remove from heat; discard bay leaf. Stir in 1½ cups milk and 1 cup light cream; add salt to taste. Cover; chill thoroughly. Makes 8 servings.

WALDORF SALAD MOLD
No final preparation

Advance preparation: Dissolve one 6-ounce package lime-flavored gelatin in 2 cups boiling water; stir in 1½ cups cold water. Chill till mixture is partially set.

In mixer bowl combine chilled gelatin and one 18-ounce can lemon pudding; beat 2 minutes with electric mixer. Stir in 2 cups diced, unpeeled apple and ½ cup chopped walnuts. Pour salad into 8½-cup mold; chill till firm. Makes 8 to 10 servings.

GRASSHOPPER CAKE

No final preparation

  **4 1-ounce squares unsweetened
    chocolate, melted**
  ½ cup boiling water
  ¼ cup sugar
  2½ cups sifted cake flour
  1½ cups sugar
  3 teaspoons baking powder
  1 teaspoon salt
  ½ cup salad oil
  7 egg yolks
  1 teaspoon vanilla
  7 egg whites
  ½ teaspoon cream of tartar
  Grasshopper Filling

Advance preparation: Blend together first
3 ingredients; cool. Sift together flour and
next 3 ingredients. Make a well in center of
dry ingredients; add oil, egg yolks, ¾ cup
cold water, and vanilla. Beat very smooth.
Stir chocolate mixture into yolk mixture.
Beat egg whites with cream of tartar till
very stiff peaks form. Carefully fold chocolate batter into egg whites. Turn into un-
greased 10-inch tube pan. Bake at 325° till
done, about 65 minutes. When done, invert
pan; cool overnight.

Next morning, remove cake from pan;
split crosswise into 3 layers. Prepare Grasshopper Filling; spread between cake layers
and on top. Chill, uncovered, 1 to 6 hours.

Grasshopper Filling: Soften 1 envelope
unflavored gelatin (1 tablespoon) in ¼ cup
cold water. Heat ½ cup green crème de
menthe with ⅓ cup white crème de cacao.
Add softened gelatin; stir till dissolved.
Cool. Prepare two 2-ounce envelopes dessert topping mix following package directions; fold in gelatin mixture. Chill till
mixture mounds, 30 minutes; stir often.

A chocolate-mint favorite

Try velvety-rich Grasshopper Cake, an im-
pressive dessert that rates high with guests
and eliminates last-minute hostess duties.

HOLIDAY DINNER

MENU
Chilled Citrus Cup
Roast Turkey   French Bread Dressing
Whipped Potatoes   Turkey Gravy
Au Gratin Onions   Broccoli Spears
Hard Rolls   Butter
Cherry-Cran Salad
Frozen Pumpkin Pie
Coffee   Milk

COUNTDOWN
FROM KITCHEN TO TABLE

Several days before dinner, prepare appetizer and pie; freeze. Day before dinner thaw turkey; follow advance preparation for dressing, onions, and salad. Thaw appetizer in the refrigerator. Select table appointments and serving dishes.

Time before serving:

4 to 5 hours Begin roasting *unstuffed* turkey according to directions on original wrap.

1 hour Bake French Bread Dressing. Set table.

50 minutes Bake onions. Peel and cook potatoes.

30 minutes Place salad on plates; chill. Start coffee.

20 minutes Cook broccoli.

15 minutes Remove turkey from oven. Heat rolls.

10 minutes Prepare turkey gravy. Whip potatoes.

5 minutes Place food in serving dishes; keep warm. Serve Chilled Citrus Cup.

Invite guests and family to table.

CHILLED CITRUS CUP
No final preparation

⅔ cup sugar
2 grapefruit, peeled and sectioned
4 oranges, peeled and sectioned
**1 15½-ounce can pineapple chunks
    with juice**
½ cup lime juice (about 4 limes)

Advance preparation: In saucepan bring sugar and 2 cups water to boiling. Simmer, uncovered, 5 minutes; cool. Add grapefruit, oranges, pineapple, and lime juice; stir lightly. Cover; refrigerate or freeze.
Before serving: Thaw frozen mixture in refrigerator overnight or at room temperature for 3 to 4 hours. Makes 12 servings.

FRENCH BREAD DRESSING
1 hour cooking time

1 cup chopped onion
½ cup sliced celery
½ cup butter or margarine
**1 8-ounce can water chestnuts,
    drained and sliced**
¼ cup snipped parsley
1 teaspoon poultry seasoning
1 teaspoon ground sage
3 beaten eggs
**1 13¾-ounce can chicken broth
    (1¾ cups)**
12 cups French bread cubes

Advance preparation: Cook onion and celery in butter till tender. Remove from heat; stir in water chestnuts, next 3 ingredients, and ½ teaspoon salt. Combine eggs, broth, and onion mixture. Add bread; toss lightly. Spoon into 2-quart casserole; cover and refrigerate. Do not stuff turkey.
Before serving: Bake casserole, covered, at 350° for 30 minutes. Uncover; bake 25 to 30 minutes longer. Makes 12 servings.

AU GRATIN ONIONS
50 minutes cooking time

        2 pounds onions, sliced and separated
            into rings (8 medium)
        2 tablespoons butter
        2 tablespoons all-purpose flour
    ⅔ cup milk
        3 ounces sharp process American
            cheese, shredded (¾ cup)
        2 tablespoons chopped canned
            pimiento
        Dash hot pepper sauce
    1½ cups fine soft bread crumbs
        3 tablespoons butter, melted

Advance preparation: Cook onions, uncovered, in boiling, salted water till tender,
12 minutes; drain. Place in 1½-quart casserole. Melt 2 tablespoons butter; blend in
flour and ½ teaspoon salt. Add milk; cook
and stir till thick and bubbly. Remove from
heat; stir in cheese, pimiento, and pepper
sauce. Pour over onions; stir. Cover; chill.
Toss crumbs with melted butter; chill.
Before serving: Bake, covered, at 325° for
25 minutes; stir. Top with crumbs; bake,
uncovered, 25 minutes more. Serves 12.

FROZEN PUMPKIN PIE
No final preparation

        1 16-ounce can pumpkin
        1 cup brown sugar
        1 teaspoon salt
        1 teaspoon ground ginger
        1 teaspoon ground cinnamon
        1 teaspoon ground nutmeg
        2 quarts vanilla ice cream
        2 9-inch graham cracker crusts
    ¼ cup chopped pecans, toasted

Advance preparation: Combine first 6 ingredients; mix well. Stir ice cream to soften;
quickly fold in pumpkin mixture. Spoon
into crusts; top with pecans. Freeze till
firm; cover and return to freezer.
Before serving: Remove from freezer about
10 minutes before serving. If desired, top
with whipped cream. Makes two 9-inch pies.

Red and white Cherry-Cran Salad, prepared
with jellied cranberry sauce, lends a tra-
ditional flavor to the holiday festivities.

CHERRY-CRAN SALAD
No final preparation

Advance preparation: Drain one 20-ounce
can frozen pitted tart red cherries, thawed;
reserve syrup. If needed, add water to syrup
to make 1 cup; bring to boiling. Remove
from heat. Add one 3-ounce package cherry-
flavored gelatin; stir to dissolve.

With fork, break up one 8-ounce can
jellied cranberry sauce; stir into cherry
gelatin till smooth. Stir in drained cherries.
Turn into 9x9x2-inch baking dish; chill till
mixture is *almost* firm.

Dissolve one 3-ounce package lemon-
flavored gelatin in 1 cup boiling water. Beat
one 3-ounce package cream cheese, softened,
with ⅓ cup mayonnaise or salad dressing;
gradually add lemon gelatin. Stir in one 8¾-
ounce can crushed pineapple, undrained.
Chill till mixture is partially set.

Whip ½ cup whipping cream; fold into
lemon mixture with 1 cup miniature marshmallows. Spread atop *almost* set cherry
layer; sprinkle with 2 tablespoons chopped
nuts. Cover; chill till firm. Serves 12.

OUTDOOR BARBECUE

MENU

Cranberry-Ham Grill
Vegetable Vinaigrette   Chive Bread
Honeydew Wedges
Lemonade   Coffee

COUNTDOWN
FROM KITCHEN TO TABLE

Several days before picnic, prepare Chive Bread; freeze. Day before barbecue, follow advance preparation for ham and salad.

Time before serving:

1¼ hours   Start fire. Make lemonade.

30 minutes   Grill ham. Set table.

20 minutes   Heat bread. Start coffee.

5 minutes   Drain salad. Place food in serving dishes on table.

Invite guests to picnic table.

CHIVE BREAD
20 minutes cooking time

   1 unsliced loaf French bread
   ½ cup butter or margarine, softened
   ⅓ cup grated Parmesan cheese
   ¼ cup finely snipped chives

Advance preparation: Slash bread in 1-inch slices, *cutting to, but not through* bottom crust. Blend together butter, cheese, and chives; spread on one side of each bread slice. Wrap loaf in foil; freeze.
Before serving: Thaw bread in foil at room temperature 2 to 3 hours. Heat on edge of grill 20 to 30 minutes; turn frequently. (Or heat in oven at 400° for 20 minutes.)

CRANBERRY-HAM GRILL
5 minutes to assemble
30 minutes cooking time

Advance preparation: Slash fat edge of 1 center-cut ham slice, 1 inch thick (1½ pounds); place ham in shallow baking dish. Combine 1 cup cranberry juice cocktail, ¼ cup orange marmalade, 1 teaspoon Worcestershire sauce, ½ teaspoon dry mustard, and ⅛ teaspoon ground cloves; pour mixture over ham. Cover and refrigerate 4 to 24 hours; turn ham occasionally.
Before serving: Drain ham; reserve marinade. Mix 2 tablespoons sugar and 1 tablespoon cornstarch; stir in reserved marinade. Cook and stir till thick and bubbly; keep warm. Grill ham over *slow* coals, 15 minutes on each side, brushing with warm sauce.
   Stir one 8-ounce can whole jellied cranberry sauce into warm sauce; pass with ham. If desired, garnish ham with orange wedges and parsley sprigs. Serves 6.

VEGETABLE VINAIGRETTE
No final preparation

Advance preparation: In shallow dish mix one 10-ounce package frozen corn and lima beans, cooked and drained; one 8-ounce can red kidney beans, drained; and 1 onion, sliced and separated into rings. Mix 1 cup clear French salad dressing with herbs and spices, ¼ cup minced green pepper, and 2 tablespoons snipped parsley; pour over vegetables. Cover; chill 6 to 24 hours.
Before serving: Drain salad. Serves 6.

Barbecuing at its best

Outdoor entertaining is fun with a make-→
ahead menu, such as Cranberry-Ham Grill, Vegetable Vinaigrette, and Chive Bread.

WEEKEND ENTERTAINING

WEEKEND MENUS

Saturday Lunch

Soufflé à la Broccoli
Tomato Wedges
Carrot and Celery Sticks
Toasted English Muffins   Butter
Banana Split Pie
Iced Tea   Milk

Saturday Dinner

Chilled Apricot Nectar
Fillet Rolls Deluxe
Buttered Peas with Water Chestnuts
Frozen Lemon Salad
Hard Rolls   Butter
Melon with Orange
Coffee   Milk

Sunday Brunch

Cran-Citrus Cup
Baked Eggs   Sausage Links
Hot Applesauce
Whole Wheat Toast   Butter
Berry Coffee Cake
Coffee   Milk

Sunday Dinner

Chilled Tomato Juice
Beef Pot Roast   Pan Gravy
Potatoes   Carrots
Lime-Pear Mold
Assorted Relishes
Brown-and-Serve Rolls
Butter   Orange Marmalade
Peach-Cream Freeze
Coffee   Milk

COUNTDOWN FROM KITCHEN TO TABLE

A few weeks before guests arrive, freeze Soufflés, Banana Split Pie, Lemon Salad, coffee cake, and Peach-Cream Freeze.

Day before entertaining, prepare Melon with Orange, Cran-Citrus Cup, Lime-Pear Mold, relishes, and stuffing for fish *(do not stuff fish)*; cover and chill.

Time before serving Saturday Lunch:

1¼ hours	Bake soufflés. Make tea.
30 minutes	Set table; slice tomatoes.
15 minutes	Prepare broccoli sauce.
5 minutes	Toast muffins. Pour beverage. Place food on table.

Time before serving Saturday Dinner:

1 hour	Stuff fish. Prepare sauce.
45 minutes	Bake fish. Set table.
20 minutes	Remove salad from freezer.
15 minutes	Start coffee. Cook peas.
10 minutes	Cut salad; place on plates.
5 minutes	Keep food warm. Serve appetizer.

Time before serving Sunday Brunch:

30 minutes	Heat coffee cake.
25 minutes	Set table. Start coffee.
20 minutes	Brown sausage. Bake eggs.
15 minutes	Warm applesauce.
10 minutes	Toast bread.
5 minutes	Keep food warm. Serve appetizer.

Time before serving Sunday Dinner:

2¾ hours	Simmer roast till tender.
1 hour	Add vegetables to roast.
30 minutes	Set table. Start coffee.
20 minutes	Unmold salad; chill.
15 minutes	Brown rolls. Prepare gravy.
5 minutes	Keep food warm. Serve appetizer.

SOUFFLÉ À LA BROCCOLI

15 minutes to assemble
1¼ hours cooking time

6 tablespoons butter or margarine
⅓ cup all-purpose flour
2 cups milk
12 ounces sharp process American cheese, shredded (3 cups)
6 eggs
½ teaspoon cream of tartar
Broccoli Sauce

Advance preparation: Melt butter; blend in flour. Add milk; cook and stir till thick and bubbly. Add cheese; stir till melted. Remove from heat. Separate eggs; beat yolks till thick and lemon-colored.

Stir cheese mixture into yolks; cool. Beat egg whites with cream of tartar to stiff peaks. Fold yolk mixture into whites. Pour into 8 *ungreased* individual (1 cup) soufflé dishes. Cover with foil; freeze.

Before serving: Set frozen soufflés in shallow pan filled with hot water to depth of ½ inch. Bake at 300° till knife inserted off-center comes out clean, 1¼ hours.

Serve with *Broccoli Sauce:* In saucepan cook ¼ cup chopped onion in 2 tablespoons butter till tender; blend in 2 tablespoons all-purpose flour. Dissolve 1 chicken bouillon cube in ½ cup boiling water; add to saucepan with 1 cup milk. Cook and stir till thick and bubbly. Stir in one 10-ounce package frozen chopped broccoli, cooked and drained; heat through. Serves 8.

This simple freezer-to-oven entrée, Soufflé à la Broccoli, prevents kitchen tasks from interrupting special weekend activities. As soufflés bake, prepare the creamy broccoli sauce.

BANANA SPLIT PIE
No final preparation

3 medium bananas
1 tablespoon lemon juice
1 baked 9-inch pastry shell, cooled
1 pint strawberry ice cream
1 cup frozen whipped dessert
    topping, thawed
  Whole maraschino cherries
2 tablespoons finely chopped
    walnuts
        • • •
  Canned chocolate sauce

Advance preparation: Thinly slice bananas; sprinkle with lemon juice and arrange on bottom of pastry shell. Stir ice cream to soften; spread atop bananas. Freeze firm.
  Spread dessert topping over ice cream layer. Top with cherries; sprinkle with nuts. Return to freezer; freeze firm.
Before serving: Remove pie from freezer and let stand at room temperature for 30 minutes. Serve with chocolate sauce.

FROZEN LEMON SALAD
No final preparation

1 8-ounce package cream cheese,
    softened
¼ cup mayonnaise or salad dressing
1 pint lemon sherbet
1 11-ounce can mandarin orange
    sections, drained
1 10-ounce package frozen peaches,
    thawed, drained, and cut up
¼ cup slivered almonds, toasted
  Lettuce

Advance preparation: In large bowl combine cream cheese and mayonnaise; beat till smooth. Stir sherbet to soften; quickly stir into cream cheese mixture. Stir in orange sections, peaches, and almonds. Turn into 8x8x2-inch baking dish. Freeze firm.
Before serving: Remove salad from freezer and let stand at room temperature for 10 to 15 minutes. Cut in squares; serve on lettuce. Makes 9 to 12 servings.

FILLET ROLLS DELUXE
15 minutes to assemble
45 minutes cooking time

2 tablespoons chopped onion
⅓ cup uncooked long-grain rice
2 tablespoons butter or margarine
1 chicken bouillon cube
1 3-ounce can chopped mushrooms,
    drained
        • • •
8 fish fillets (2 pounds)
3 tablespoons butter or margarine
3 tablespoons all-purpose flour
1½ cups milk
½ cup dry white wine
4 ounces process Swiss cheese,
    shredded (1 cup)
  Paprika

Advance preparation: In saucepan brown onion and rice in 2 tablespoons butter, 5 to 8 minutes; stir often. Add 1 cup water, bouillon cube, and ¼ teaspoon salt. Bring to boiling; stir. Cover; cook over low heat till rice is fluffy, 20 to 25 minutes. Stir in mushrooms. Cover and chill.
Before serving: Season fish with salt; spread with rice mixture. Roll up fillets; secure with wooden picks. Place, seam side down, in 10x6x1¾-inch baking dish.
  In saucepan melt 3 tablespoons butter; blend in flour, ¼ teaspoon salt, and dash pepper. Add milk and wine. Cook and stir till thick and bubbly; pour over fillets. Bake, uncovered, at 400° for 35 minutes. Sprinkle with cheese and paprika. Continue baking till fish flakes easily with fork, 5 to 10 minutes more. Makes 8 servings.

MELON WITH ORANGE
No final preparation

Advance preparation: Combine ½ cup light corn syrup; ¼ cup frozen orange juice concentrate, thawed; and ¼ cup orange-flavored liqueur. In deep bowl place 4 cups honeydew balls and 4 cups cantaloupe balls. Pour syrup mixture over all. Cover and chill, stirring once or twice. Serves 8.

CRAN-CITRUS CUP
No final preparation

   1 cup sugar
   ½ teaspoon grated orange peel
   1 cup orange juice
   2 cups fresh cranberries
   2 16-ounce cans grapefruit
       sections, undrained

Advance preparation: In saucepan combine sugar, orange peel, and orange juice. Bring to boiling, stirring to dissolve sugar; boil, uncovered, for 5 minutes. Stir in fresh cranberries; cook till skins pop, about 5 minutes. Remove from heat; gently stir in undrained grapefruit sections. Cover and chill thoroughly. Makes 8 servings.

BERRY COFFEE CAKE
35 minutes cooking time

   1 cup sifted all-purpose flour
   2 tablespoons sugar
 1½ teaspoons baking powder
   ½ teaspoon salt
   ¼ cup butter or margarine
   1 beaten egg
   ⅓ cup milk
   ½ of one 10-ounce package frozen
       strawberries, thawed (½ cup)
   ¼ cup orange marmalade
   ¼ cup sugar
   3 tablespoons all-purpose flour
   ¼ cup butter or margarine

Advance preparation: Sift together first 4 ingredients; cut in ¼ cup butter till crumbly. Mix egg and milk; add to dry ingredients. Stir till moistened. Spread in 8x8x2-inch baking pan. Blend undrained berries with marmalade. Spoon over batter.

Mix ¼ cup sugar and 3 tablespoons flour; cut in ¼ cup butter till crumbly. Sprinkle atop cake. Bake at 400° for 30 to 35 minutes. Cool 10 minutes; remove from pan. Cool thoroughly. Wrap in foil; freeze.
Before serving: Heat frozen cake in foil at 350° for 30 to 35 minutes. Open foil during last 10 minutes of heating.

LIME-PEAR MOLD
No final preparation

   1 16-ounce can pear halves
   1 3-ounce package lime-flavored
       gelatin
   1 2-ounce envelope dessert topping
       mix
 1½ cups small curd cream-style
       cottage cheese
   1 envelope unflavored gelatin
       (1 tablespoon)

Advance preparation: Drain pears, reserving syrup; add water to syrup to equal 1 cup liquid. Dissolve lime gelatin in 1 cup boiling water; stir in reserved syrup mixture. Chill till partially set.

Slice 3 of the pear halves; arrange pears, pointed end down, around side of 5½- or 6½-cup mold; pour in ½ cup lime gelatin. Chill till almost set. Dice remaining pears. Add to remaining lime gelatin; keep at room temperature. Spoon over chilled gelatin; chill till almost set.

Prepare topping following package directions. Beat cheese with electric mixer till smooth; fold into topping. Soften unflavored gelatin in ¼ cup cold water; heat and stir over hot water till dissolved. Stir into cheese mixture. Pour over gelatin in mold. Chill till firm. Makes 8 servings.

PEACH-CREAM FREEZE
No final preparation

   1 22-ounce can peach pie filling
   1 15-ounce can sweetened condensed
       milk
   1 8¾-ounce can crushed pineapple,
       drained
   ¼ cup lemon juice
   ¼ teaspoon almond extract
   ½ cup whipping cream

Advance preparation: In large mixing bowl combine first 5 ingredients. Whip cream; fold in peach mixture. Spoon into 9x5x3-inch loaf pan. Freeze till firm.
Before serving: Unmold; slice. Serves 8.

make-ahead Storage Techniques

With good storage you can preserve all the delicious flavor, appearance, texture, and nutrition that you put into a make-ahead recipe. The techniques involve wrapping and refrigerating or freezing (and thawing) the food. Do these properly and you'll have perfect foods to serve.

Start by wrapping the food correctly. This seals in the flavor and moisture and keeps out air. Moisture-vapor-proof materials are designed specifically for this purpose. There are several styles from which to choose. One is the rigid container made of plastic, glass, metal, or heavily waxed cardboard. These containers include lids which form a tight seal. (If a covered casserole dish is used for freezing, put tape around the lid to make a tight seal.) The other style is the flexible wrappings such as heavy foil, clear plastic wrap and bags, and laminated paper. Fold the edges together to seal this wrapping. Freezer tape is needed to secure the fold in laminated paper and clear plastic wrap if put in the freezer.

When deciding which material to use for wrapping food, think ahead to how the food will be used. If a coffee cake is to be warmed before serving, wrap it in foil. If a casserole is to be reheated, put the casserole mixture

Wrap prepared foods with moisture-vaporproof materials before freezing or refrigerating to preserve the best flavor, texture, and appearance.

into a freezer-to-oven dish. Then the food can be taken directly from the freezer to the oven without thawing or transferring it to another container.

Wrap and refrigerate or freeze foods immediately after cooking. However, if there is a large volume of hot food that might raise the temperature inside the appliance or a dish too hot to wrap, cool it quickly by placing the pan of food in ice-cold water. Then wrap and refrigerate or freeze. Avoid cooling foods at room temperature.

When you are ready to use the food, thawing is usually not necessary, for most foods can be put directly into serving dishes or into the oven. However, if a food should require thawing, it is best to allow extra time for it to thaw in the refrigerator.

Refer to the refrigerator and freezer charts on the following pages for specific instructions on how to prepare foods for refrigerating or freezing, how long to store foods, and how to thaw or prepare for serving.

REFRIGERATOR STORAGE

Refrigeration is a simple, efficient way to store foods. For best results, observe these rules: Adjust the refrigerator temperature between 35 and 40 degrees, and place foods in their specially designed compartments where the temperature and air flow are adapted best to suit them. Follow the chart below when preparing food for the refrigerator and use the food within the time given for the best quality.

REFRIGERATOR CHART		
Food	**Preparation for refrigerating**	**Storage time**
Casseroles	Cool quickly. Cover and refrigerate.	1 to 2 days
Dairy products	Cover and refrigerate promptly.	
Butter and margarine	Wrap or cover tightly. Refrigerate.	2 weeks
Cheese	Wrap tightly. Refrigerate.	
Hard (Parmesan, Cheddar)	Wrap tightly. Refrigerate.	Several months
Soft (cream, Camembert)	Wrap tightly. Refrigerate.	2 weeks
Cottage cheese	Cover and refrigerate.	3 to 5 days
Milk and cream	Cover and refrigerate.	3 to 5 days
Eggs	Store in refrigerator with large end up.	1 week
Whites	Store in covered container. Refrigerate.	1 to 2 days
Yolks	Cover with cold water. Cover and refrigerate.	1 to 2 days
Fruit	Leave unripe fruit at room temperature.	
Apples	Refrigerate ripe fruit uncovered.	1 week
Apricots, avocados, grapes, nectarines, pears, peaches	Refrigerate ripe fruit uncovered.	3 to 5 days
Bananas	Do not refrigerate.	
Berries and cherries	Refrigerate fruit whole without washing or removing the stems.	1 to 2 days
Canned fruits and juices	Cover and refrigerate in original container.	
Citrus fruits	Store in cool room or refrigerator.	1 week
Dried fruit, uncooked	In warm weather, cover and refrigerate.	2 months
cooked	Refrigerate in covered container.	2 days
Melons	Store in cool room or refrigerator.	1 week
Pineapple	Wrap tightly in clear plastic. Refrigerate.	1 to 2 days

Food	Preparation for refrigerating	Storage time
Gravy and broth	Cover; refrigerate promptly.	1 to 2 days
Meats	Refrigerate all meat in coldest section.	
Bacon	Refrigerate in original wrap.	5 to 7 days
Cold cuts, frankfurters	Refrigerate in original wrap.	3 to 5 days
Cooked meats	Cool quickly. Wrap and refrigerate.	1 to 2 days
Fish	Wrap and refrigerate.	1 to 2 days
Ground meat	Refrigerate in original wrap.	1 to 2 days
Ham, halves	Refrigerate in original wrap.	3 to 5 days
slices	Wrap tightly. Refrigerate.	1 to 2 days
whole	Refrigerate in original wrap.	1 week
Pork (fresh)	Refrigerate in original wrap.	2 days
Poultry, uncooked	Wrap loosely and refrigerate.	1 to 2 days
cooked	Remove stuffing, if used, as soon as possible. Cool quickly and refrigerate separately.	1 to 2 days
Roasts, steaks, chops	Original wrap is sufficient for 1 or 2 days. Rewrap for longer storage.	3 to 5 days
Sausage (raw pork)	Refrigerate in original wrap.	2 to 3 days
Variety meats	Wrap loosely and refrigerate.	1 to 2 days
Pies	Refrigerate cream pies promptly.	
Salad oil	Refrigerate to prolong storage.	
Stews and soups	Cool quickly. Cover and refrigerate.	1 to 2 days
Stuffings	Remove from leftover meat immediately. Refrigerate, covered, separately from meat.	1 to 2 days
Vegetables	Sort out bruised, soft, and decaying ones.	
Asparagus, beans, Brussels sprouts, rhubarb, mushrooms, peas, corn, spinach, tomatoes	Store, covered, in crisper section of the refrigerator or in clear plastic bags.	1 to 2 days
Artichokes, beets, broccoli, cauliflower, cucumber, eggplant, lettuce, summer squash	Store, covered, in crisper section of the refrigerator or in clear plastic bags.	3 to 4 days
Cabbage, carrots, celery, green pepper, radishes	Store, covered, in crisper section of the refrigerator or in clear plastic bags.	1 week or more
Potatoes, sweet potatoes, onion, hard-rind squash	Store in cool, dry room.	1 week or more

FREEZER STORAGE

Freezing is an excellent way to prolong storage of foods. When using a freezer, keep the temperature at zero degrees or lower. Add hot foods in small amounts so the temperature will not rise above zero. (Consult your freezer booklet for the recommended amount of hot foods to add.)

When preparing food for the freezer, follow the directions in the freezer chart and use the food within the time suggested for top quality. Season foods lightly before freezing and adjust the seasonings when reheating. When frozen with food mixtures, cloves, garlic, pepper, and celery may become stronger while onion, salt, and chili powder may become weaker. When packaging foods, divide the amount into meal-sized portions before wrapping. Label each

package with contents; any special instructions for serving, such as adding seasonings or topping when reheating; number of servings; and the date frozen or the date by which it should be used.

There are a few foods that should not be frozen because freezing changes their flavor or texture. These are bananas, hard-cooked egg whites, boiled frostings, fried meats, luncheon meats, boiled potatoes in mixtures (substitute rice instead), green onions, radishes, cucumbers, lettuce, and salad greens. Vegetables such as green pepper, celery, and tomatoes do not freeze satisfactorily for salad use. However, if they are for cooked mixtures, freezing is satisfactory. Mayonnaise or sour cream may separate if frozen.

FREEZER CHART

Food	Preparation for freezing	How to thaw	Storage time
Breads: Baking powder biscuits	Bake biscuits as usual; cool. Seal biscuits in freezer container, or wrap in foil. Seal, label, and freeze.	Place biscuits in foil wrapping on baking sheet. Thaw in 250° to 300° oven about 20 minutes.	2 months
Doughnuts	Fry; cool. Wrap, seal, label, and freeze.	Reheat in oven.	2 to 4 weeks
Muffins	Bake as usual; cool. Seal in freezer containers, or wrap in foil and seal. Freeze.	Thaw in package at room temperature 1 hour or in 250° to 300° oven till warmed.	2 months
Yeast bread	Bake bread as usual; cool quickly. Wrap, label, and seal. Freeze.	Thaw, wrapped, at room temperature for 3 hours.	2 months
Yeast rolls	Use either plain or sweet dough recipe. Bake as usual; cool quickly. Wrap in foil, seal, and label. Freeze at once.	Thaw baked rolls in foil package at room temperature or in 250° to 300° oven about 15 minutes. Use rolls at once.	2 months
	Or partially bake at 325° about 15 minutes; do not let brown. Cool quickly, wrap, label, and seal. Freeze at once.	Thaw frozen, partially baked rolls 10 to 15 minutes at room temperature. Unwrap; bake at 450° till hot, about 5 to 10 minutes. Serve rolls at once.	2 months
Cakes: General	*Baked:* Remove from pan; cool thoroughly. If you frost cake, freeze it before wrapping. Wrap; seal. If desired, place in sturdy container. Return to freezer at once. (Unfrosted cakes freeze better. Filled cakes may become soggy.)	Thaw in wrapping at room temperature (2 to 3 hours for large cakes; 1 hour for layers). If frosted or filled, thaw loosely covered in the refrigerator.	Unfrosted 6 months Frosted 2 months

Food	Preparation for freezing	How to thaw	Storage time
Cupcakes	Bake as usual; cool. If frosted, freeze before wrapping. Seal in freezer container or wrap and seal. Return to freezer. (Unfrosted ones freeze better.)	Thaw, wrapped, at room temperature for 40 minutes. If frosted, thaw loosely covered in the refrigerator.	2 months
Sponge and angel food cakes	Bake as usual; cool thoroughly. If frosted, freeze before wrapping. Then wrap and seal. If desired, place in sturdy container. Return to freezer at once.	Thaw in package 2 to 3 hours at room temperature. If frosted, thaw loosely covered in the refrigerator.	1 month
Cake frostings and fillings	*Recommended for freezing:* Frostings of confectioners' sugar and fat, cooked-candy type with honey or corn syrup, fudge, penuche, fruit, and nuts are good to freeze. Seal in containers; freeze. *Not recommended:* Soft frostings, boiled icing, seven-minute frosting, and cream fillings are not desirable to freeze.	Thaw in refrigerator.	2 months
Cookies: Unbaked	Pack dough in freezer containers; seal. *Not recommended:* Meringue-type cookies do not freeze well.	Thaw in package at room temperature till dough is soft. Bake cookies as usual.	6 to 12 months
	Bar cookies. Spread dough in baking pan; wrap, seal, label, and freeze.	Bake without thawing.	6 to 12 months
	Refrigerator cookies. Shape into rolls; wrap, seal, label, and freeze.	Thaw slightly at room temperature. Slice rolls; bake.	6 to 12 months
Baked	Bake cookies as usual; cool thoroughly. Pack in freezer containers with waxed paper between layers and in air space. Seal, label, and freeze.	Thaw in package at room temperature.	6 to 12 months
Pastry	Pastry and graham cracker shells freeze well. Roll out dough; fit it into pie plates. Bake, if desired. Prepare crumb shells as usual. Wrap, seal, freeze.	Thaw baked pastry at 325° for 8 to 10 minutes. Unbaked frozen pastry is baked the same as fresh pastry.	2 months •
Pies: Fruit, general	*Unbaked:* Treat light-colored fruits with ascorbic acid color keeper to prevent darkening. Prepare pie as usual but don't slit top crust. Use glass or metal pie plate. Cover with inverted paper plate. Wrap and seal. If desired, place in sturdy container. Freeze at once.	Unwrap frozen pie; cut vent holes in top crust. Without thawing, bake at 450° to 475° for 15 to 20 minutes, then at 375° till done. *Berry, cherry:* Unwrap; cut vent holes in top crust. Without thawing, bake at 400° till done.	
	Baked: Bake as usual in glass or metal pie plate. Cool. Package as above.	Thaw in package at room temperature or in 300° oven.	2 months
Apple, unbaked	Use firm varieties of apples. Steam slices 2 minutes, cool, and drain; or treat with ascorbic acid color keeper. Prepare and package as above.	Unwrap; cut vent holes in top crust; bake at 425° till done, about 1 hour.	2 months
Peach, unbaked	To keep color bright, treat with ascorbic acid color keeper or lemon juice. Prepare and package as above.	Unwrap frozen pie; cut vent holes in top crust. Bake, without thawing, at 400° till pie is done, about 1 hour.	2 months
Chiffon	Chocolate and lemon freeze well.	Thaw in refrigerator.	2 weeks
Deep-dish fruit pies	Use deep pie plate.	Bake or thaw frozen pie using the directions given above for two-crust pies.	2 months

Food	Preparation for freezing	How to thaw	Storage time

Main dishes:
Casseroles:
   Poultry, fish,
   or meat with
   vegetable or
   pasta
	Cook meat till tender. Cook vegetable and pasta till *almost* tender. Cool mixture quickly. Turn into pint or quart freezer containers, or into freezer-to-oven baking dish. Cover tightly. Seal, label, and freeze.	If frozen in freezer-to-oven baking dish, uncover. Bake at 400° till hot through, about 1 hour for 2-cup quantities and 1¾ hours for 4-cup quantities. Or steam over hot water in top of double boiler, stirring frequently but gently, till hot.	2 to 4 months

Creamed dishes:
   Chicken, turkey,
   fish, or
   seafood
	Cool quickly. Freeze any except those containing hard-cooked egg whites. Don't overcook before freezing. Use fat sparingly when making sauces. This helps prevent separation when reheating. Cover tightly. Seal, label, and freeze.	Heat frozen mixture in top of double boiler, stirring occasionally. If sauce separates, stir till smooth. About 30 minutes is needed to thaw and heat 2-cup quantities.	2 to 4 months

Meatballs with tomato sauce	Cook till done; cool quickly. Ladle into jars or freezer containers, allowing 1-inch headspace. Seal, label, and freeze.	Thaw in saucepan over low heat or in top of double boiler. Stir occasionally, being careful not to break up meatballs. Or defrost overnight in refrigerator and heat in saucepan.	3 months
Meat pies and scalloped dishes	Cook meat till tender. Cook vegetables till *almost* tender. Cool quickly. Put in freezer-to-oven baking pan or dish. Top with pastry or freeze pastry separately. Wrap tightly. Seal, label, and freeze.	Bake frozen pies with pastry topper till hot through and crust is browned, about 45 minutes for 2-cup quantities and 1 hour for 4-cup quantities.	2 to 3 months

Roast beef, pork,
   poultry, and
   other cooked
   meats
	Prepare as for serving. (Do not freeze fried meats or poultry.) Remove excess fat and bone. Cool quickly. Wrap tightly. It is best to freeze small pieces or slices; cover with broth, gravy, or sauce. Wrap tightly, seal, label, and freeze.	Thaw large pieces of meat in the refrigerator before heating. Heat meat with sauce in top of a double boiler.	2 to 4 months

Spaghetti sauce	Cool sauce quickly; ladle into jars or freezer containers, allowing about 1-inch headspace. Seal, label, and freeze.	Heat over low heat in top of a double boiler, stirring frequently but gently.	2 to 3 months
Vegetables: Baked beans with tomato sauce	Chill mixture quickly. Package in moisture-vaporproof container. Cover tightly.	Partially thaw in package. Heat casserole in the oven or in top of a double boiler.	6 months
Spanish rice	Use long-grain rice. Cook till rice is tender, but not mushy. Cool quickly; package. Seal, label, and freeze.	Heat in top of double boiler till hot through, about 50 minutes. Add a little water, if needed.	3 months
Stews and soups	Select vegetables that freeze well. Omit potatoes. Onions lose flavor. Green pepper and garlic become more intense in flavor. Omit salt and thickening if stew is to be kept longer than 2 months. Do not completely cook vegetables. Cool quickly. Wrap, seal, label, and freeze.	Heat quickly from frozen state. Do not overcook. Separate with fork as it thaws. Do not stir enough to make the mixture mushy.	2 to 4 months
Sandwiches	*These fillings freeze well:* Cream cheese, hard-cooked egg yolk, sliced or ground meat and poultry, tuna, salmon, and peanut butter. Spread slice of bread with softened butter; spread with filling. Place second buttered bread slice atop. Wrap tightly. Seal; label with contents. Freeze. *These are not recommended:* Lettuce, celery, tomatoes, cucumber, watercress, whites of eggs, jelly, and mayonnaise.	Thaw sandwiches in wrapping at room temperature about 3 hours. Serve immediately after the sandwiches are thawed.	2 weeks

INDEX

A-B

C